BECK INSTITUTE
FOR COGNITIVE THERAPY

THE USE OF
ALTERNATIVE MODES
FOR COMMUNICATION
IN PSYCHOTHERAPY

THE USE OF ALTERNATIVE MODES FOR COMMUNICATION IN PSYCHOTHERAPY

The Computer
The Book
The Telephone
The Television
The Tape Recorder

By

DAVID LESTER, Ph.D.
Richard Stockton State College
Pomona, New Jersey

CHARLES C THOMAS • PUBLISHER
Springfield • Illinois • U.S.A.

Published and Distributed Throughout the World by
CHARLES C THOMAS • PUBLISHER
Bannerstone House
301-327 East Lawrence Avenue, Springfield, Illinois, U.S.A.

This book is protected by copyright. No part of it
may be reproduced in any manner without
written permission from the publisher.

© *1977, by* CHARLES C THOMAS • PUBLISHER
ISBN 0-398-03655-1
Library of Congress Catalog Card Number: 77-1712

With THOMAS BOOKS *careful attention is given to all details of manufacturing and design. It is the Publisher's desire to present books that are satisfactory as to their physical qualities and artistic possibilities and appropriate for their particular use.* THOMAS BOOKS *will be true to those laws of quality that assure a good name and good will.*

Printed in the United States of America
R-1

Library of Congress Cataloging in Publication Data
Lester, David, 1942-
 The use of alternative modes for communication in psychotherapy.

 Bibliography: p.
 Includes index.
 1. Psychotherapy--Audio-visual aids. 2. Bibliotherapy. I. Title.
RC480.5.L44   616.8′914′028   77-1712
ISBN 0-398-03655-1

INTRODUCTION

THIS book examines the use of different media for communication in counseling and psychotherapy. Traditionally, the patient or client and the psychotherapist or counselor sit in the same room and talk to each other. Communication is direct and takes place on different levels, both verbal and nonverbal.

In recent years, there has been an increasing use of alternative modes of communication in psychotherapy. For example, the rise of suicide prevention centers led to an expanded use of counseling by telephone, primarily because this mode of communication was the most apt for the clientele for whom the centers were designed. Counseling by telephone changes the nature of the psychotherapeutic relationship drastically. Visual cues between client and counselor are eliminated, and there is a radical shift in the power balance of the relationship.

The aim of this book is twofold. First, the book surveys the various ways in which alternative modes of communication have been utilized in psychotherapy and counseling. In particular, the uses of the telephone, the tape recorder, the book, the computer, and the television or videotape in psychotherapy are reviewed. Each review surveys the many uses to which these alternative modes of communication have been put and, in addition, focuses upon the unique characteristics that each alternative mode of communication brings to the psychotherapeutic relationship.

The second aim is to reflect upon the implications of the use of these alternative modes of communication for our understanding of the nature of psychotherapy and the reasons for its success. For example, Chapter 5 is a discussion of the use of the tape recorder in counseling; research is reviewed exploring the utility of seating institutionalized juvenile delinquents in a room by themselves in order for them to talk out loud while being recorded on tape. The counselor never provides any feedback to the delinquents about the content of what they say during these sessions. If such a technique has a psychotherapeutic effect, to what can we attribute its success and what does its success mean for our understanding of the nature of psychotherapy? These issues are addressed in Chapter 6.

As each chapter is written to be a self-contained review of the literature, the reader may feel free to begin with any chapter.

CONTENTS

	Page
Introduction	v

Chapter

1. TELEVISION AS A MEDIUM FOR PSYCHOTHERAPY 3
2. THE USE OF THE TELEPHONE IN COUNSELING AND CRISIS INTERVENTION 14
3. THE USE OF THE COMPUTER IN PSYCHOTHERAPY AND COUNSELING 41
4. PSYCHOTHERAPY BY PRINTED WORD 70
5. THE TAPE RECORDER AND COUNSELING 92
6. EPILOGUE 100

Index 107

THE USE OF ALTERNATIVE MODES FOR COMMUNICATION IN PSYCHOTHERAPY

Chapter 1

TELEVISION AS A MEDIUM FOR PSYCHOTHERAPY

THE use of television and videotape systems has become increasingly popular with psychotherapists in recent years. The greater part of the interest has been in the use of videotape to record the behavior of a patient or group of patients in order to confront them with this view of their behavior. Although this use of television is important and may have important consequences for the psychotherapeutic process, it is not relevant here. What is of interest is the use of television as a *medium for communication* in which a patient and a psychotherapist communicate with each other via a television circuit.

A few examples will clarify this distinction.

NATHAN'S TRACCOM

Nathan et al. (1968) have described a technique which they called TRACCOM (Televised Reciprocal Analysis of Conjugate Communication). A psychiatrist interviewed a suicidal alcoholic who was an inpatient in a psychiatric hospital. There was one interview lasting an hour for each of thirteen weeks. Each participant sat in his own room which was equipped with a television camera and television screen. In order to see and hear the other person each participant had to repeatedly press a hand-held switch. (In other reports, the switch was a footswitch, and there have been reports in which two switches were used, one for the sound and one for the visual channel.) To receive a maximally clear picture and sound of the other, the participant had to press at a rate of 120 per minute; to blot out the other, all that was necessary was to lower his rate of pressing the switch.

Nathan et al., recorded the rate of switch pressing and had

the psychotherapist and the patient complete questionnaires after each session. The data is not especially relevant to the use of this technique for psychotherapy, but it is suited for research investigating the process of psychotherapy. For example, in the first six sessions the psychotherapist increased his rate of pressing during the course of the session. In the latter seven sessions he decreased his rate of pressing during the sessions to the point where he could not see or hear the patient for much of the time. Thus, two distinct periods in the therapeutic relationship were apparent.

The psychotherapist expected the situation to feel unreal but was surprised to find that it did not seem that way. He noted the elimination of status differences (for example, the psychotherapist did not sit behind a desk) and the equalization of power (each could obliterate the other by changing the switch pressing rate). The psychotherapist felt that the patient cooperated and used the customary defense mechanisms and modes of adaptation found in face-to-face psychotherapy. Incidentally, the technician in charge of the equipment became involved in the process and took the patient's side against the psychotherapist.

Although a patient soon forgets about the need to press the switch, the movement necessary may facilitate thinking and free association, perhaps in the way that having a patient walk around a group while talking frees thinking. Lindsley (1969) sees the technique as providing a method of matching psychotherapist and patient using a nonconscious measure of interest in each other, for determining the optimal length of psychotherapy sessions, and for feedback (both *after* and *during* the session) to the psychotherapist about the interest level of his patient.

DWYER'S IATV

Dwyer (1973) has described an interactive television system (IATV) initially set up between Massachusetts General Hospital and Logan International Airport in Boston to permit psychiatric and medical interviews between doctors at the hospital and patients at the airport. Although useful for psychiatric emergencies with patients, the system has been used primarily for psychiatric evaluations and counseling of the airport staff and their families. Dwyer and his staff have conducted diagnostic interviews, prescribed drugs, conducted crisis intervention, and held individual and group psychotherapy sessions with the system.

The system has been expanded and now provides consultation to groups such as high school teachers, counselors, and probation officers, and diagnostic interviews for prisoners.

Many psychotherapists first react negatively to the system. Dwyer felt that these feelings were based primarily on previous experience with television in which the viewer is passive. Once the psychotherapist and patient adjust to the fact that this is an interactive television process, the negative reactions quickly disappear.

Economically the system is excellent. It permits the distant patient to interact with a psychotherapist or counselor more easily and cheaply. It permits agencies and locales with poor psychiatric and psychological resources to "share" a centralized counseling center, thereby utilizing psychotherapists efficiently. Since operating costs are low and treatment more accessible, the system has great potential for early detection and treatment of problems. It is ideal for screening patients and reducing the need for hospitalization for purposes of observation.

Dwyer reported that the degree of personal contact with the patient was full. The psychotherapeutic transactions possessed the richness of face-to-face sessions. The two participants were "in touch" despite the mediation by electronics.

Dwyer felt that some patients can benefit more from televised sessions than from face-to-face sessions, especially schizophrenics and younger patients (children and adolescents). Although some patients showed initial anxiety in the situation, all adjusted, and paranoid patients did not incorporate the television into their delusional thinking.

WILMER'S TELEVISED MONOLOGUES

Wilmer (1970) has adolescents in inpatient treatment for drug-related problems make a videotape for their psychotherapist.

The adolescent sits in a television studio by himself and records a fifteen minute tape which he can review. If he wishes, he can erase the tape or he can show it to his psychotherapist. The adolescents appear to like this. (The unit uses videotaping a great deal, and the adolescents are used to it.) Only a few erase the tape. (Incidentally, new staff are offered the technique to introduce themselves to other staff and most refuse.) The patient reviews the tape with his psychotherapist.

The tape provides a clinical case record. It also permits the patient to reveal his inner speech because there is no therapeutic prodding. For some patients, inhibitions are lessened and free association and regression are shown. Transference is more easily expressed, since no adult is around to inhibit the patient. Wilmer felt that the monologues were diagnostic, informational, and therapeutic; he is experimenting with their use throughout treatment.

DINOFF'S STANDARDIZED VIDEOTAPE INTERVIEW

Dinoff et al. (1969) have constructed a videotape interview in which the interviewer asks fifteen questions, mainly nondirective, of a patient. The patient's responses can be recorded. The interview is thereby standardized and useful for research purposes where elimination of interviewer bias is crucial.

Waters (1975) used the interview and found no differences in college students in their galvanic skin response, self-rated anxiety or amount spoken when they were given both the videotape interview and the face-to-face interview.

OTHER USES OF TELEVISION AND VIDEOTAPE

The Training of Counselors

Two systematic techniques for training counselors have appeared in recent years. In *microcounseling* (Ivey, 1972) the counselor learns one counseling skill at a time, practicing with volunteer clients. Videotapes of counselors displaying the skill are available, and the videotapes of counselors attempting to develop this skill can be viewed, compared, and discussed. The important features of this method are the emphasis on learning one skill at a time and self-observation on videotape. Higgins et al. (1970) have utilized the technique to teach specific skills to patients, for example, teaching married couples to move away from confrontive conversations to sharing conversations.

In *interpersonal process recall* (Kagan and Krathwohl, 1967), the counselor conducts a session with a volunteer client which is videotaped. The interview is watched by an observer. The counselor leaves; then the observer interrogates the client about what took place in the interview. A second observer may simultaneously interrogate the counselor in a separate locality. Both interrogations are audiotaped for later study. Interpersonal process recall is insight-oriented. Although this method was designed for training counselors, it has also been found to speed up the process of psychotherapy for the patient.

Stimulating Psychotherapy

Videocassettes of psychotherapy and real-life situations have been used to stimulate psychotherapy. One example is a cassette of a family argument, followed by the mother of the family talking to the audience about her true feelings may be used to stimulate a group discussion in children about the divorces in their families (Cowan and Kinder, 1975).

Catanzaro (1967) recorded a psychodrama of a conflict situation (marital or employment) acted out by patients in front of a group of alcoholic patients, who then discussed the problems portrayed while reviewing the tape.

Clinical Records

Videotaping of patients has been used for data collection. Samples of patient behavior can be recorded throughout treatment and then filed as part of the case record, providing a much richer report than mere written documents (Cornelison,

1963). Such tapes can also be used for training counselors, for example, by showing a patient at different stages of treatment (Macdonald, 1974).

Katz and Itil (1974) have argued that the use of videotaped samples of patient behavior can assist research. When ratings of patients' behavior are required, the use of videotaped samples permits the use of more judges, the use of expert judges, and the control of the independent variables (such as the stage of treatment or the particular treatment group), since the samples can be presented to the judges in random orders. Katz and Itil reported a study of the effects of thioridazine and thiothixene on patients using such a methodology and they found subtle but important differences in the action of the two drugs. Katz and Itil stressed the usefulness of a standardized interview for research purposes, and Dinoff's work (reviewed above) is relevant here.

Supervision of Counselors

Videotaping has often been used to observe patients; now it is used especially with patient-counselor interaction for purposes of supervising the counselor. Videotaping provides a much richer source of feedback for the counselor and supervisor than mere audiotaping (Gruenberg et al., 1969).

Confronting Patients

The major use of videotaping has been to confront patients with audiovisual samples of their own behavior (Bailey and Sowder, 1970). The aim may be to focus on personal and interpersonal distress, and may focus on specific problems such as attempting to increase the concordance of verbal and nonverbal communications skills. Marvit et al. (1974) reported a successful demonstration of videotaped playback of group psychotherapy sessions used to change the self-confidence facade that delinquents have. The delinquents became more aware of how they appeared to others. The aim may be to train instrumental skills such as teaching impression management for potential job applicants. Paden et al. (1974) reported an effort (which failed) to improve the eating behavior of patients using videotape playback of their eating behavior. In a variant of self-confrontation, Resnick et al. (1973) confronted a suicidal patient with scenes from the emergency room procedures involving him and his family's reactions to his suicide attempt.

Diagnosis

Haworth and Menolascino (1967) videotaped play sessions with children to facilitate observation of their behaviors and differential diagnosis. The use of videotape permitted the use of many judges who were able to replay at will the records of the behavior. Bellino (1973) has suggested that videotaping a person when he believes he is alone may facilitate the detection of malingering.

Models

Videotaped illustrations have been used to provide models for behavior. Krumboltz et al. (1967) showed high school students a film of vocational counseling to motivate them to use the counseling resources. Striefel (1972) argued that television could be used to provide models and to give instruction to mentally retarded children (who appear to enjoy watching television). Striefel and Eberl (1974) were able to get retarded persons to obey commands given over the televison. Greer and Callis (1975) motivated alcoholics for treatment by showing them videotaped interviews with recovered alcoholics. Rathus (1973) used videotaped models to make assertiveness training more effective. Strupp and Bloxom (1973) showed films (of a troubled man seeking psychotherapy) in order to motivate lower class patients for group psychotherapy by reducing their misconceptions about psychotherapy, thereby decreasing their defensiveness and sense of threat. Strupp and Bloxom presented evidence to indicate that the technique was successful. Macdonald et al. (1972) had people watch videotapes of sensitivity-training groups. Although the viewers were motivated to join such groups by this exposure, they did not change in the degree of self-disclosure that they showed after watching the videotapes.

Televising Psychotherapy

Shostrom (1968) explored the effects of televising a group in psychotherapy and showing it on local television. Not only did the viewers who wrote in to the television station report that they found the program growth-producing, but the patients felt that the televising of the group accelerated their progress. (Since the sessions were pre-recorded, the patients could watch the broadcast.) None of the patients were concerned about the loss of privacy.

Stoller (1967) recorded group psychotherapy with psychiatric patients and televised these sessions to patients in other wards. The chronic regressed patients in the groups were stimulated while on camera and participated more than when in regular groups. The recognition from fellow patients subsequently was reinforcing and again stimulated them. During the sessions, the patients' psychotic verbalizations decreased and their spontaneity increased. The effects of this might be compared to the effects of psychodrama and support Mowrer's (1964) plea that public confession of mental illness and misdeeds ought to be more psychotherapeutic than private confession to a psychotherapist. The patients who viewed the sessions also seemed helped by them, though this result was not studied in detail. (Incidentally, the television cameramen and technicians were patients too.)

Miscellaneous Uses

Woody and Schauble (1969) used videotaped sequences to present the fear-invoking stimulus to the patient in systematic desensitization sessions.

Forrest et al. (1974) have prepared an electronic textbook of psychiatry, which has psychiatric interviews included, for the training of medical students.

Rader and Schill (1973) have shown students in a course on projective testing a patient being tested with the tester interpreting the protocol "blindly." The students then met the patient and the tester in person in the classroom. Rader and Schill felt that this procedure helped to overcome the prejudice that some students feel toward projective testing.

CONCLUSIONS

It is clear that television and videotaping has been used in a variety of innovative ways in counseling and psychotherapy, although, many of these uses have not involved using the television as a medium for direct communication. Television has been used mainly to supplement psychotherapy.

However, it is clear that the use of television for patient-psychotherapist communication is possible and that when it is used as the medium for communication it has the result of minimizing status differences between patient and psychotherapist. In some arrangements, such as Nathan's TRACCOM, it results in the equalization of power between patient and psychotherapist, because the patient can "tune-out" the psychotherapist. These results of changing the mode of communication between the patient and the psychotherapist are shown more clearly in the use of the telephone as the mode of communication and they have been studied in greater detail in that mode.

REFERENCES

Bailey, K., and Sowder, E.: Audiotape and videotape self-confrontation in psychotherapy. *Bull Psychol*, 74:127-137.
Bellino, T.: The Ganser syndrome. *Int J Offender Ther*, 17:136-137, 1973.
Catanzaro, R.: Tape-a-drama in treating alcoholics. *Q J Stud Alcohol*, 28:138-140, 1967.
Cornelison, F.: Samples of psychopathology from studies of self-image experience. *Dis Nerv Syst*, 24:133-135, 1963.
Cowan, C., and Kinder, W.: Split Screen. *Newsweek*, 21:58-59, 1975.
Dinoff, M., Clark, C., Reitman, L., and Smith, R.: The feasibility of videotape interviewing. *Psychol Rep*, 25:239-242, 1969.
Dwyer, T.: Telepsychiatry. *Am J Psychiatry*, 130:865-869, 1973.

Forrest, D., Ryan, J., Glavin, R., and Merritt, H.: Through the viewing tube. *Am J Psychiatry, 131*:90-94, 1974.

Greer, R., and Callis, R.: The use of videotape models in an alcohol rehabilitation program. *Bull Rehabil Counsel, 18*:154-159, 1975.

Gruenberg, P., Liston, E., and Wayne, G.: Intensive supervision of psychotherapy with videotape recording. *Am J Psychother, 23*:98-105, 1969.

Haworth, M., and Menolascino, F.: Videotape observations of disturbed young children. *J Clin Psychol, 23*:135-140, 1967.

Higgins, W., Ivey, A., and Uhlemann, M.: Media therapy. *J Counsel Psychol, 17*:20-26, 1970.

Ivey, A.: *Microcounseling*. Springfield, Thomas, 1971.

Kagan, N., and Krathwohl, D.: *Studies in Human Interaction*. East Lansing, Educational Publication Services, 1967.

Katz, M., and Itil, T.: Video methodology for research in psychopharmacology. *Arch Gen Psychiatry, 31*:204-210, 1974.

Krumboltz, J., Varenhorsh, B., and Thoresen, C.: Nonverbal factors in the effectiveness of models in counseling. *J Counsel Psychol, 14*:412-418, 1967.

Lindsley, O.: Direct behavioral analysis of psychotherapy sessions by conjugately programmed closed-circuit television. *Psychother Psychosom, 6*:71-81, 1969.

Macdonald, A., Games, R., and Mink, O.: Film-mediated facilitation of self-disclosure and attraction to sensitivity training. *Psychol Rep, 30*:847-857, 1972.

Macdonald, D.: Group characteristics of alcoholics. *Ann N Y Acad Sci, 233*:128-135, 1974.

Marvit, R., Lind, J., and McLaughlin, D.: Use of videotape to induce attitude changes in delinquent adolescents. *Am J Psychiatry, 131*:996-999, 1974.

Mowrer, O.: *The New Group Therapy*. New York, Van Nostrand, 1964.

Nathan, P. Smith, S., and Rossi, M.: Experimental analysis of a brief psychotherapeutic relationship. *Am J Orthopsychiatry, 38*:482-492, 1968.

Paden, R., Himelstein, H., and Paul, G.: Videotape versus verbal feedback in the modification of meal behavior of chronic mental patients. *J Consult Clin Psychol, 42*:623, 1974.

Rader, G., and Schill, T.: Blind test interpretation to overcome student resistance to projective techniques course. *J Pers Assess, 37*:213-216, 1973.

Rathus, S.: Instigation of assertive behavior through videotape mediated assertive models and directive practice. *Behav Res Ther, 11*:57-65, 1973.

Resnick, H., Davison, W., Schuyler, D., and Christopher, P.: Videotape confrontation after suicide. *Am J Psychiatry, 130*:460-463, 1973.

Shostrom, E.: Witnessed group therapy on commercial television. *Am Psychol, 23*:207-209, 1968.

Stoller, F.: Group psychotherapy on television. *Am Psychol,* 22:158-162, 1967.
Striefel, S.: Television as a language training medium with retarded children. *Ment Retard,* 10(2):27-29, 1972.
Striefel, S. and Eberl, D.: Imitation of live and videotaped models. *Educ Train Ment Retard,* 9:83-88, 1974.
Strupp, H. and Bloxom, A.: Preparing lower class patients for group psychotherapy. *J Consult Clin Psychol,* 41:373-384, 1973.
Waters, T.: Further comparison of videotape and face-to-face interviews. *Psychol Rep,* 41:743-746, 1975.
Wilmer, H.: Use of television monologue with adolescent patients. *Am J Psychiatry,* 126:1760-1766, 1970.
Woody, R. and Schauble, P.: Desensitization of fear by videotapes. *J Clin Psychol,* 25:102-103, 1969.

Chapter 2

THE USE OF THE TELEPHONE IN COUNSELING AND CRISIS INTERVENTION*

IN the course of the last two decades, there has been a tremendous increase in the use of the telephone as a medium for counseling. The stimulus for this development has had two main sources: First, the suicide prevention movement, which grew after the opening of the suicide prevention center in Los Angeles in the 1950s, adopted the telephone as the primary mode of treatment as a result of its accessibility. The individual in crisis, no matter where he is, can usually get to a telephone to call for help. Furthermore, the telephone offers a number of advantages over traditional modes of counseling, in particular the relative anonymity it affords the distressed individual. He can seek help without having to identify himself.

The second stimulus came from the development of poison information centers. Again, the telephone is the ideal mode here because of its immediacy and accessibility. If a person accidentally (or intentionally) ingests some chemical, immediate counseling as to antedotes and treatment can be obtained. Here, the telephone is being used as a way of transmitting information quickly.

These two services provided a model for immediate counseling and information-giving twenty-four hours a day by trained staff, and recently the model has been applied to a number of other areas.

---

*This paper was presented at MIT, January, 1976, sponsored by AT&T.

THE UTILIZATION OF THE TELEPHONE IN COMMUNITY SERVICES

Before proceding further, it would be useful to reconsider and describe briefly some of the uses to which the telephone has been put as an instrument of counseling and advising.

(1) The telephone has always been the major treatment mode of the suicide prevention center. In fact, many centers offer nothing but the availability of counseling by telephone.

(2) The crisis intervention center started when many suicide prevention centers soon found that they were being asked to help people in all kinds of crises, not merely suicidal crises. Accordingly, some centers changed their orientation toward more general crisis intervention and other centers were set up expressly for the purpose of general crisis intervention.

(3) Teen hot lines began when telephone counseling services oriented themselves to particular groups of the population. The most common of these are those directed toward teenagers. These teen hot lines function in much the same way as crisis intervention centers except that the kinds of problems that they handle differ. Many teen hot lines do not attempt to provide twenty-four hour service. Rather they are open for counseling in the late afternoons and evenings.

(4) Another population that has been selected for special concern is the elderly. Rescue, Inc. in Boston has run a service for senior citizens in which one call is placed each day to the members. This serves as a protection in case they are ill or there is an emergency. If there is no answer to the call, a volunteer makes a visit to the person's home. Furthermore, the calls are made by senior citizens, so social contacts are initiated and renewed in the process of maintaining the service. The service in Boston is free. In New York City, there is a service which is financed by fees from the participating senior citizens. This commercial service differs from the Boston

service in that it restricts the socializing aspects of the service. The service in New York limits calls to about a minute and serves mainly a protective function in case of illness.

(5) Some services have been established to help individuals with particular needs and problems. For example, Rescue, Inc. in Boston started a special telephone counseling service for homosexuals, with a supporting clinic service. Nowadays services exist for abortion counseling, counseling victims of rape, counseling parents who have a history of abusing their children, and so on.

(6) Other services have proceeded in a more general direction. The Suicide Prevention and Crisis Service of Buffalo opened a problems-in-living service, which tried to encourage people to call with any kind of problem.

(7) The telephone has also come into use as a means to follow up patients discharged from psychiatric facilities. For example, the Mid-Missouri Mental Health Center in Columbia made follow-up telephone calls to the former patients of the center's alcoholism treatment program.

(8) Another growing area of telephone counseling is that provided by the drug hot lines. These provide information about drugs and their effects, and counseling to those involved with drugs. Not only can they provide general counseling, but they can also help the individual who is currently either on a "bad trip" as a result of the drugs he has ingested or who is in a state of acute panic.

(9) In the information-giving area, the poison control center is available in many communities to provide immediate counseling on treatment procedures after the ingestion of chemicals of all kinds. These centers were, on the whole, originated by pediatricians to aid in the treatment of children who ingest poisons. However, there is now a shift in focus among many of these centers. It has become increasingly obvious that in many cases of "accidental" poisonings, there are self-destructive tendencies at work. Furthermore, the devel-

opment of suicide prevention centers and drug hot lines has meant that these services must work very closely with the poison control centers to facilitate treatment.

(10) One way in which information can be used to help the community is through the rumor control center. These services were primarily motivated by the riots of the 1960s and the need to dampen down the rumors that accompany such social upheavals. Now, they have extended their information-giving service to other areas of community concern.

(11) A recent development has resulted from the cooperation between radio stations and local community groups. In Call For Action, originated by the radio station WMCA in New York City, trained counselors endeavored to help listeners with specific kinds of problems, such as garbage removal, rat and pest control, low-standard housing, voter registration, consumer fraud, traffic safety, pollution, taxes, and so on. Different radio stations have occasionally focussed upon particular problems: WMCA in New York on housing; WWDC in Washington, D.C. on garbage removal.

(12) Doctor Lloyd Moglen, a psychiatrist, started a program on a radio station, KQED in San Francisco, in which listeners could call in with problems. Dr. Moglen counsels them while other listeners hear the conversations. His program differs from the typical radio station call-in programs in that his aim is counseling.

(13) Recently, both Seattle and Boston have opened a service called Tel-Med which contains a library of tape-recorded messages on more than one hundred illnesses and medical problems. Access is via the telephone, and the messages tell about the history of the illness and discuss treatment procedures. In Chicago, a similar system has been set up for doctors who can dial into a network that will put them in touch with specialists from all over the country to advise them on problem patients.

(14) Finally, there exists a growing number of minimal services that nonetheless are related to the kinds of services

that I have described above: the Dial-A-Prayer service, Wake-Up Services, and so on.

The range of services in which the telephone plays an important and central part is quite large and the telephone has demonstrated that it is particularly suitable for the goals of these services. If a community need is apparent, then a telephone counseling service can be set up in a relatively short period of time and relatively cheaply. The service it provides, once it has been advertized, is available to everyone, since people either possess a telephone or have easy access to one. When the community no longers needs such a service, it can be dismantled easily.

The proliferation of such services raises some serious issues. Is it better to have so many separate services or are they better when localized in one agency? Can quality control be assured when so many unlicensed and uninspected services exist? One central agency, with trained and supervised staff, would provide better quality counseling.

Yet would victims of rape, for example, call a general counseling service? Doesn't the provision of a special service, directed toward them and manned by sympathetic counselors, perhaps victims of rape themselves, facilitate their use of the service?

One possible solution is to provide separate telephone numbers and initiate individual advertizing campaigns, but to have the lines situated in the same agency. The Suicide Prevention And Crisis Service in Buffalo at one point had its counselors answer four different services, each with its own telephone number and advertizing program (a suicide prevention service, a teen hot line, a problems-in-living service, and a drug hot line service). In this case, however, it proved difficult to have counselors switch from service to service quickly, to turn from a seriously depressed elderly citizen who was considering suicide to a teenager who does not know how to ask out the girl who sits near him in class. Perhaps it makes most sense to coordinate services (and if possible to locate them together) but to have separate groups of counselors counseling on each service.

A second issue that the proliferation of telephone counseling services has raised is whether any counselor can counsel any caller. Must a counselor be a homosexual to counsel homosexuals, a rape victim or a female to counsel rape victims, a teenager to counsel teenagers? Or can any competent and trained counselor handle any type of client and any type of problem? To be frank, there are no empirical data that pertain to this issue, and opinions differ. The trend is, however, when community needs arise, for specific interest groups to initiate the service, which results in like-counseling-like.

THE UTILIZATION OF THE TELEPHONE IN PSYCHOTHERAPY

The telephone is also being used in an increasingly large number of ways to facilitate counseling and psychotherapy by qualified professionals engaged in individual face-to-face psychotherapy.

For example, Robertiello (1972) has reported upon two cases of psychoanalysis in which, during a temporary inability of the patient to visit the psychoanalyst's office (due to travel and illness), the psychoanalytic sessions were continued by telephone. Robertiello reported that the use of the telephone made no difference in one case (where much of the psychoanalysis consisted of discussion of the patient's dreams), and in the second case actually facilitated the psychoanalysis. In this latter case, the transference had been so disruptive that the patient had been unable to stand being in the same room with the psychoanalyst. Her emotions interfered with the integration of insights into her ego. The telephone sessions enabled her to experience the emotions and, in addition, to reflect upon the transference.

Beebe (1968) has reported on the use of the telephone to begin the integration of the schizophrenic patient into his family. Beebe regarded the first goal to be the return of the patient to involvement in his difficult family situation, rather than isolating him from it for a while. Obviously, physically returning him to his family is too stressful. For the schizophrenic, the telephone often provides the right amount of distance. The call permits contact without closeness. It serves to curb the fantasies which take over when there is no exchange. In return, the family feels involved and permitted to help undo whatever harm they have done to the patient.

Beebe reported a case of an acute schizophrenic psychosis in a sailor. The patient had been forced into the service by his parents who had wanted to get rid of him. Early in training, he became anxious, confused, and felt that he had sinned. At the height of his confusion, he believed that he had killed his mother. The call home was a great relief to him, and he became quite lucid and free of psychosis after the call home.

Owens (1970) has demonstrated the effectiveness of inducing hypnosis by telephone. He called up a number of his patients (Owens is a dentist) with whom he had used hypnosis before, and used a standard induction procedure to induce a mild level of hypnosis. In all cases he was successful. He was also successful with two patients whom he had never previously hypnotized. Owens' intent was simply to explore whether hypnotic states could be induced by telephone. However, his patients did report feelings of relaxation and a reduction in dental pain after the hypnotic induction and so the procedure may have some utility.

The telephone has been used to follow-up discharged alcoholics (Catanzaro and Green, 1970), to speed up consultation between the patient and the counselor, and to enable case supervision for counselors by their supervisors (Wolf, et al., 1969). Chiles (1974) has used the telephone contact to reinforce behavior modification procedures with patients. A call may be made each day lasting a few minutes so that a counselor can have the patients report briefly on aspects of their behavior, such as eating behavior, the consumption of alcohol, hostile behavior with relatives, and so on. The telephone contact serves to maintain the behavior modification program and reinforces the patient's self-image, thereby facilitating the patient's continuation of the behavior modification regimen.

Miller (1973) surveyed a number of psychiatrists and found that 97 percent used the telephone for handling emergencies, 45 percent used the telephone as a planned adjunct to face-to-face psychotherapy, and 19 percent used the telephone as the primary mode of treatment. The psychiatrists differed in how easy they found the telephone to be as a mode of communication.

Miller noted that it is important for a psychotherapist to know his own reaction to the mode of counseling, the reaction of his patients, and the suitability of the particular problem to the mode. Miller noted, for example, that, in general, psychiatrists found depression most difficult to handle over the telephone while anxiety was comparatively easy.

THE UNIQUE CHARACTERISTICS OF TELEPHONE COUNSELING

As experience with the use of the telephone in counseling and psychotherapy grew, it became apparent that such counseling had unique characteristics not shared by other modes of counseling.

Client Control

When a client walks into a counselor's office, the counselor has most of the power. There may be a receptionist for the client to deal with. Once past the receptionist, the client faces a counselor who usually sits behind a desk. There may be a difference in status that is reflected in the dress of the counselor, or in the difference between the luxury of the office of the counselor and the client's home. The client cannot remain anonymous; even if he gives a false name, he can be recognized subsequently. The client is often required to give out personal information about himself while, of course, this is not necessary for the counselor. Furthermore, it is difficult for the client to terminate the contact. He must stand up and leave the office, which allows the counselor time to intercede and prevent the client's departure. As Williams and Douds (1973) have pointed out, it is very easy for a face-to-face counseling contact to be anxiety-provoking and humiliating for a client.

In contrast, the client has much more control in a telephone contact. The client may remain absolutely anonymous. He need give no information about himself, and he remains unseen. (Even if a counselor were able to obtain permission from the telephone company to trace the call, this process could take over an hour, and the client could easily be using a public telephone.) The client can terminate the contact quite easily by hanging up on the counselor. (This method of abrupt termination is often a most immediate and effective comment on a counselor's performance.)

This equalization of control often produces anxiety in the counselor at first. More importantly, it has a facilitative effect on the client. The client who is anxious or who feels threatened may never walk into a counselor's office, but he may call the counselor on the telephone. On the telephone, the client can maintain a feeling of freedom and a sense that he cannot be hurt or victimized.

This equalization of power is not only useful for a client in crisis who is calling a counselor for the first time but also for patients in psychotherapy. MacKinnon and Michels (1970) reported a case of a phobic housewife who was only able to reveal disturbing thoughts about the psychotherapist when she was forced to call him during a snowstorm which prevented her from traveling to his office. This patient subsequently sought a telephone session when she again had thoughts that were difficult to relate.

Client Anonymity

The client can remain anonymous when talking to a counselor via the telephone. The possibility of hiding one's identity can facilitate greater self-revelation and openness on the part of the client. The anonymity minimizes the client's feeling that he might be ridiculed, abused, censured, or hurt as a result of the counselor's evaluation of him. The facilitative effect of anonymity is illustrated by the common assumption that it is easier to talk about one's problems to a stranger than to an acquaintance.

Positive Transference

The counselor can also remain anonymous, and this has advantages. In face-to-face counseling, any fantasy that the client may have about the counselor is checked against reality, and the chances are high that the counselor may not live up to the fantasy. A distressed individual may not, in his state of distress, be able to tolerate the shattering of his illusions, for those illusions may give him a sense of security that permits him to make the contact for counseling.

The telephone counselor may also fail to live up to the client's fantasy, but he will be far more like the client's ideal than the face-to-face counselor, since the client is presented with only the voice of the counselor and not with visual cues.

If the client can make of the counselor what he *will*, he may also be able to make of the counselor what he *needs* (Williams, 1971). This may facilitate moving the client out of his distressed state.

Of course, there are dangers in allowing a client to dwell too long in a world of fantasy. Situations can easily occur where the development of fantasy works to the disadvantage of the client (and of the counselor), and the client must be forced to face reality. However, a skilled counselor can use the positive transference to help the client move to a stronger psychological state and subsequently move the patient to a realistic acceptance of what is happening in the counseling process.

Reduced Dependency

The anonymity of the counselor has an additional advantage for the clinics which employ a number of telephone counselors. These clinics usually decide that counselors should remain anonymous, using a first or assumed name only. The counselors are told to discourage clients from becoming dependent upon any one counselor. This has the result that the client becomes dependent upon the *clinic* rather than on a particular *counselor*. In this situation, when a counselor leaves the clinic temporarily or permanently, the client is much less upset than in situations where dependency has been centered on one particular counselor. This advantage is of particular use when the clients are suicidal, for such clients often respond to a vacation on the part of their psychotherapist or his leaving the area by attempting suicide.

Accessibility

Most people have access to a telephone and the cost is low. This accessibility is critical for clients in crisis (especially a suicidal or homicidal crisis) and for the elderly and infirm. Many individuals are bedridden or too weak or senile to visit a counselor for face-to-face psychotherapy. Telephone counseling is often the only source of counseling for such people.

MacKinnon and Michels (1970) noted this advantage with cases from a private psychotherapy service. Psychotherapy was maintained in one case with a female client twice weekly while she went to Nevada to obtain a divorce and with another female client for three months while she remained in bed at the order of her obstetrician.

Immediacy

There is an immediacy to the telephone and many clinics maintain twenty-four telephone counseling services. Thus, an individual in distress can immediately locate a counselor ready to provide aid. This feature of telephone counseling agencies has been used by psychotherapists who advise their patients to utilize such services at nights, on weekends, and while the psychotherapist is on vacation. It is helpful, of course, if the psychotherapist works with the agency in formulating a treatment plan for patients in these situation.

Other Properties

Miller (1973) has noted five properties of the telephone that are pertinent to its use in counseling. The spatial property of the telephone breaks down the barriers between the counselor's office and the client, a point analogous to the accessibility noted above. Miller also noted that the telephone permits a more distant relationship than face-to-face counseling, but one which is quite intimate (since the voice of the patient is close to the ear of the counselor and vice versa).

The temporal property of the telephone means that the counselor can be called at any time of the day or week (although, of course, the counselor can put barriers in the way of complete accessibility, by having an unlisted number or by disconnecting his telephone). The patient is not limited to the counseling sessions for his contact with the counselor.

A third property of the telephone is that it is single channeled, that is, communication is restricted to audition. This restricts communication to verbal communication and allows for greater freedom for fantasy.

A fourth property of the telephone is that it is a machine, a concrete object and rather impersonal to relate to and through. However, recent studies indicate that patients do not find it too impersonal to have a computer administer a psychiatric intake interview, and in fact, a good proportion of patients preferred to have their interview conducted by a computer rather than a human (Greist et al., 1973). The fact that the telephone is a machine may not necessarily make the patient uncomfortable.

A fifth and final property of the telephone noted by Miller is that it is dyadic. Usually, conversations are between two people, and, although this can be modified, telephone contacts are more often dyadic than face-to-face contacts.

Miller noted how these properties of the telephone may result in characteristic uses. The spatial property appeals to patients with dependency and oral needs, who can reassure themselves that support is at hand. Ambivalent patients (such as some schizophrenics) may use the telephone to maintain distance and control in the therapeutic relationship. Hostile patients may be able to express their emotions because they feel safer doing so at a distance. The spatial property commonly makes the counselor feel that he has less control of the counseling relationship, and that he is open to unreasonable demands by patients for his time. (Miller noted that under some circumstances it might be appropriate to charge the patient for telephone contacts.)

The temporal property appeals to impulsive patients who cannot tolerate anxiety. The psychotherapist often experiences anger with these patients, and Miller suggested that the psychotherapist set firm limits on how much use of the telephone he will accept.

The single-channel property appeals to patients who want to remain anonymous or protect themselves from the psychotherapist. They do not trust the psychotherapist, they may merely be exploring the possibility of psychotherapy, or they may find it less embarrassing, anxious, or shameful to discuss particular problems over the telephone. The lack of visual cues may distress psychotherapists who utilize nonverbal methods of communication. It may impede effective evaluation of the patient's state, and it may lead to misleading fantasies on the part of the psychotherapist.

The mechanical property of the telephone may appeal to patients such as obsessive neurotics and schizophrenics. On the other hand, Miller felt that counselors dislike the impersonal quality of the telephone. Miller felt that the dyadic property appealed to people who wished to shut other people out from their communications with a psychotherapist, but in fact individual face-to-face psychotherapy is no different in this respect.

Miller noted that the psychotherapist can be active in his use of the telephone. He can use it to give support to insecure and unstable patients between regular psychotherapy sessions. He can instruct impulsive patients to call whenever they feel that they may act upon their impulses, and he can instruct patients who block in psychotherapy to call when they recall the thought. He can utilize the telephone for patients who have difficulty in talking about particular issues face-to-face. He can also utilize the telephone to contact significant others in order to bring them into the treatment process or to evaluate the patient more accurately.

PROBLEMS ASSOCIATED WITH TELEPHONE COUNSELING

Of course, along with the advantages of the telephone as a mode of counseling, several disadvantages and dangers exist. An allusion was made above about the dangers of the counselor or psychotherapist allowing his fantasizing about the client to get out of hand. I argued that it may, under some circumstances, be useful for the client to be able to fantasize about the counselor. It is never useful for the counselor to fantasize about the patient and to cease to be anchored in reality. Similarly, mention was made above of the eventual dangers of the client's fantasies about the counselor. At some point during the counseling process, these fantasies must be brought out, examined, and adjusted to reality.

Brockopp (1970) has noted that it is easy for counselors to slip into a conversational mode with the client rather than remain in a psychotherapy mode. The telephone is strongly associated in people with the conversational mode, and it easy for the counselor to revert to old habit patterns when using the telephone. In addition, although the telephone allows greater distance between client and counselor (such as anonymity), it also is an intimate encounter. The counselor may be relaxed in a comfortable chair and the voice of the client is close to his ear. This intimacy can facilitate the appearance of the conversational mode.

(Incidentally, this tendency to slip into a conversational mode is a particular problem for counselors working in a clinic that maintains a twenty-four hour telephone counseling service. Occasionally, a counselor will work a night-shift alone, and it is a poor practice to sleep between calls, for the counselor can easily resent being awakened from a deep sleep to handle a client in crisis. The awake counselor is alone and can easily come to welcome calls from clients. They help to pass the time. A counselor under these conditions may seek to prolong conversations with clients, simply because he has nothing to do when the call is over. Under these circumstances, counseling often degenerates into conversation.)

Should the counselor slip into the conversational mode, the psychotherapeutic process is minimized, distorted, or eliminated: The counselor's objectivity is reduced; confrontation is less likely; the client's anxiety may be reduced to such an extent that he no longer feels a need to work on his problem; and the false assumption develops that what is taking place is the process of psychotherapy.

PROBLEMS ASSOCIATED WITH TELEPHONE COUNSELING SERVICES

Many of the problems that arise with telephone counseling are not a result of the mode of counseling. Many agencies that now provide telephone counseling services use nonprofessionals to answer the telephones, and it is this use of nonprofessionals (rather than the use of the telephone) that causes problems. Lamb (1970) has discussed some of the typical problems that nonprofessionals have in counseling. For example, a common problem is the fantasy of omnipotence, with its variants: "But all I'm doing is listening!", "If I talk about it, it may happen" (the power-of-positive-thinking error), and "But he's manipulating me" (the who's-in-charge-here error).

Although volunteers and nonprofessionals have been utilized in mental health settings for a long time (Gruver, 1971), the proliferation of telephone counseling services has accelerated their use. A telephone counseling service requires about sixty to eighty volunteer counselors in order to maintain a twenty-four hour service seven days a week in a major city. The majority of these counselors are usually nonprofessionals who have received at most twenty-four hours of training and who receive perhaps an hour of supervision each week.

This use of nonprofessionals has raised the issue of whether they perform worse than, the same as, or better than professionals. McGee and Jennings (1973) have argued, for example, that nonprofessional counselors can counsel with higher levels of empathy than professionals. On the other hand, McColskey (1973) has argued that, if it is believed that clinical training has any value, then it is absurd to argue that relatively untrained people can perform better than trained people. With a rigorous selection process, adequate training, and good supervision, perhaps some nonprofessionals can do a good job with most clients. But can they handle all kinds of crises, and can they be trusted to behave professionally? The answer to the first question is clearly no, since most services have to employ professionals as back-up consultants around the clock. The answer to the second question is also probably no.

The American Association of Suicidology recently debated the issue of whether it is ethical for telephone counseling services to tape-record calls without the clients' knowledge. The majority of centers considered it to be unethical. At the center where I worked, calls were tape-recorded both for supervision of the counselor and for research purposes. There were calls where the counselor fell asleep while a client was talking and where a counselor began a call by laughing at a client who told him that she felt like killing herself. (The counselors had to turn on their own tape recorders to tape-record calls, and what was most surprising was that neither counselor erased their performances.)

Most centers would argue that their counselors would not make these errors. Yet the majority of centers do not monitor their counselors by day, let alone by night. The regular staff have no idea of their counselors' actions.

Furthermore, nonprofessional telephone counselors have no concept of professional behavior. They easily get emotionally and intimately involved with clients. When counselors voluntarily leave a telephone counseling service (or are fired), cases exist where they have contacted clients, who formerly called the telephone counseling service, in order to maintain a relationship with the client. The mental health professions have problems enough today with unethical behavior on the part of psychotherapists. The problems with nonprofessionals are much greater.

There is nothing technically wrong with one member of a community interacting in a destructive way with another member of a community. There is something greatly wrong when one of those individuals is affiliated with a mental health agency.

As a result of these kinds of problems, I (Lester, 1973) have advocated that nonprofessionals be closely supervised, more closely than any other group of mental health workers. And furthermore, I have advocated the replacement of hordes of part-time volunteer nonprofessional telephone counselors by a few full-time well-payed highly-trained paraprofessionals whose performance can be accurately monitored.

Problem Callers

Telephone counseling services attract clients who present problems for the counselor that are less common in face-to-face counseling. These services have stimulated empirical and theoretical interest in these "problem callers." The most noteworthy example here is the obscene caller. Many telephone counseling services receive calls from males who wish to talk to a female while masturbating. In addition, particular problems are raised by the chronic caller (the client who calls several times each day), the silent caller (who calls but refuses to say anything), and the nuisance or prank caller. The management of these kinds of problems has been discussed by Lester and Brockopp (1973).

Supplementary Services

Telephone counseling services are limited in the service they can provide, and it is important for such services to recognize that telephone counseling is often not sufficient to provide assistance to clients. Hoff (1973) has discussed the importance of an adequate follow-up, including subsequent medical and psychiatric help, personal contact by telephone or in person, and contact with the significant others of the client. Richard and McGee (1973) have described the development of an outreach team that has the training and mobility to make home visits. Such a service is a most useful addition to a telephone counseling service engaged in crisis intervention work.

Furthermore, crisis intervention can be traumatic for the counselor and the counselor may well need support and advice and the opportunity to share his responsibility for the client.

The Chronic Caller

Lester (1971) has discussed one kind of caller that most telephone counseling services have experienced — the chronic caller. These clients call the service regularly: Cases exist of clients calling five times a day and spending as much as thirty-five hours a week talking to counselors. Since telephone counseling services typically employ a large number of telephone counselors, a chronic caller may talk to a different counselor each time he calls. It is difficult for each counselor to report problems and progress with the caller to other counselors, and it is difficult for the full-time staff to formulate and implement a coherent and rational treatment plan. The lack of supervision of telephone counselors in most agencies means that it is difficult to enforce a treatment plan once it is formulated. (At the center where I worked, one counselor who was in many respects an excellent counselor refused to limit the calls from a particular chronic caller as the treatment plan recommended. He said that to do so was inhumane!) Furthermore, clients often gratify needs of telephone counselors that are not necessarily relevant to their functioning as counselors. To be specific, one chronic caller to the teen hot line in Buffalo was a teenage girl whose chronicity was able to develop partly because the male counselors at the center liked talking to this attractive-sounding girl. The sexual gratification for both the client and the counselors was readily apparent.

This particular case presented a difficult problem for the professional staff. Various solutions were tried, such as limiting her calls to one counselor and inviting her to the center so that she could meet the counselors (and so that they could meet her) in order to try to remove some of the fantasy from the involvement. However, several months later the problem had still not been solved, and the girl was still a chronic caller.

The chronic caller has been focussed upon here because the telephone counseling service itself creates this problem. The psychological condition of the chronic caller may have deteriorated as a result of his dependency upon the service. His dependencies may have been more appropriately distributed prior to his involvement with the center, and they are certainly not useful distributed *after* the development of his chronic dependency upon the center. Centers often justify their continued involvement with chronic callers by hoping that the telephone contact reduces the chance that the client will have to be hospitalized in a psychiatric facility. The center sees itself as helping the client to continue to exist in the community. There is, however, usually no evidence that this is the case.

It is of utmost importance to examine those problems that institutions create, in addition to examining those that they solve. Innovations in any field, and perhaps especially in the area of mental health, often have drawbacks and create new problems. These problems are then often dealt with by creating additional services. Such a proliferation of services might also be supported for ecomomic reasons, for thereby a large number of people are kept employed. But if this is the chief advantage of such a state of affairs, then the presentation of false evidence to support its continued existence should be avoided.

The provision of mental health services with easy access may reinforce behaviors in the population that are not advantageous to mental health. It may, for example, reinforce the obsessive preoccupation with our psychological mood and behavioral symptoms. It may encourage people to disclaim responsibility for their unhappy relatives and friends who have problems in living. It may facilitate the labeling of people as psychiatrically disturbed, thus encouraging them into the career of a psychiatric patient (Scheff, 1966). It is an open question as to whether mental health services increase either the level of mental health in the community or the level of happiness.

The existence of the chronic caller, therefore, is the kind of problem that should make telephone counseling services examine the rationale for their continued existence and the effectiveness of their treatment programs.

Agencies and Their Continued Existence

Brockopp (1973) noted that agencies often become less concerned with their function than with their continued existence. They lose sight of the client and focus more on their furniture and the procurement of a larger budget for the next fiscal year. Brockopp urged that all innovative agencies should be set up with the understanding that they would be disbanded in say five years, transferring the experimental programs that worked to other agencies. In this way, the agency would focus on its function rather than its continued existence.

This point is an important consideration for all kinds of agencies, but telephone counseling services merit special attention. Telephone counseling services are often established in response to temporary community needs. As community needs change, the services face identity crises. What should the service do? Continue or disband? Baizerman (1975) has discussed this issue for teen hot lines which now deal with different kinds of problems than those for which they were formed. Ten years ago teenagers called with crises: drug highs, runaways, the need for a place to bed-down for the night, police arrest, military draft counseling, and so on. These were "real crises" to the counselors. Today, calls to teen hot lines are connected with loneliness, family conflict, and dating problems. The "crisis" has gone out of the crisis call. Teen counselors often wonder these days why they are counseling, whom they should serve, what they should do? The services have lost their purpose. Some argue that the services should close their doors and hang up their telephones; others are searching for new purposes for the services to pursue.

THE RESEARCH STIMULUS FROM TELEPHONE COUNSELING SERVICES

The development of telephone counseling services has stimulated a good deal of research in a variety of areas.

The growth of the suicide prevention movement in the 1950s led to the recognition that a decision model was needed by which counselors could estimate simply the probability that a client who was calling would kill himself. This led to the development of simple scales to predict suicidal risk (Lester, 1970). There are a number of other behaviors for which simple prediction scales would be of use. It would be most useful, for example, if it could be predicted whether an individual was likely to assault or murder others. However, without the stimulus of counseling agencies to deal specifically with assaultive behavior, the construction of such predictive scales has been slow.

A number of reports have appeared concerning the selection of telephone counselors (Lester and Williams, 1971; Tapp and Spanier, 1973) and the particular personality traits that characterize such volunteers. There has also been a good deal of work on how to evaluate the effectiveness of the telephone counseling services and their counselors (Lester, 1972; McDonough, 1975).

Telephone counseling services provide a convenient setting in which to conduct research on the effectiveness of counseling. The derivation of objective criteria to determine whether clients are helped by counseling has proved difficult. How can psychological improvement be measured? In telephone counseling services, limited but objective criteria is often found. Did the client accept the referral that was suggested? For example, did the client show at some clinic for a face-to-face psychotherapy session as arranged (Slaikeu et al., 1973; Buchta et al., 1973).

Telephone calls can be recorded. Thus, it is a little easier with telephone counseling services to use the technique of simulated calls in which some actor plays a patient with a particular kind of problem. The call can be recorded and subsequently examined to see whether the telephone counselor functioned adequately (for example, Bleach and Claiborn, 1974). Since most telephone counseling services use a crisis counseling model, it is easy to listen to calls and rate the counselors for their technical effectiveness in following the guidelines for handling crises (Fowler and McGee, 1973) and the dimensions of empathy and genuineness that telephone counselors are supposed to show (Carothers and Inslee, 1974).

It is probably true to say that telephone counseling services have been more aware of the importance of evaluating their effectiveness than have other mental health agencies.

Comment

It is clear from this review that the telephone provides an important tool for the counselor in helping his clients. The qualities of the telephone make it the treatment of choice for particular clients and for many other clients at some point in their counseling. It poses problems for the counselor, but adequate training and experience should enable the counselor to employ the telephone effectively in counseling.

Telephone counseling services have been an important influence in the provision of treatment of psychological problems. The services have provided needed services for communities and, in addition, have stimulated a good deal of discussion about the role and the purpose of mental health agencies. The services have also stimulated a good deal of research on the selection, training, and evaluation of counselors. In many respects, therefore, telephone counseling services have had a welcome catalytic effect on the thinking of mental health professionals.*

APPENDIX: A CALL FROM A CHRONIC CALLER

In order to illustrate a telephone counseling call taken at a crisis counseling center, two calls from a chronic caller are reproduced below. The chronic caller and the problems that he presents have been discussed in detail elsewhere (Lester and Brockopp, 1973) and so there is no need to go into the issues of case management here. The intent here is merely to give the reader a glimpse into telephone counseling.

The client was married and fifty-two years old. She called the counseling service 188 times during an eight month period. Her contact with the service terminated when she moved to another state. She will be called Jane.

Almost all of Jane's calls were interrupted by her husband or her employer's arrival on the scene, or by her whenever a suggestion was made to her by the counselor. She was depressed but she appeared to dislike talking about her problems and being questioned about them by the counselors. All she appeared to want was to reiterate her problems. Jane was able to control the telephone counseling so as to achieve her aims. If we can believe her letter to the service, written after she had left the area, she had benefited from her contact with the service, and so she was perhaps able to shape her own counseling especially to her own needs.

The two calls transcribed below were received from her after she had been calling the service for about two months. The first call was interrupted by her employer. The second was ended by Jane as soon as the counselor made a recommendation to Jane about what she should do.

After Jane had left the area, she wrote a note to the service. This note is reproduced after the two calls.

---

*This chapter has elaborated and updated ideas discussed by the author in previous publications (Lester 1974a, 1974b; Lester and Brockopp, 1973).

The First Call 4:20 p.m.

This is Miss Smith.
Miss Smith, this is Jane.
Hi Jane.
I'm sorry —uh— but somebody walked in the office before and I couldn't talk. The same thing may happen again.
Right. O.k. Well, I'm here if you want to talk —uh— you called earlier today, right?
Yes and they were too busy to talk.
Oh yeah. Well we've had some calls on - I mean we had some information on T.V. and on radio and when we get a spot announcement well we get more calls. I think that's what happened when you called.
I see. Uh-huh. Well anyhow, uh — oh I thought maybe — now I can't talk again. I'll have to call you.
O.k. Jane. Fine. We'll be here.

Second Call: 12:50 p.m. Two days later

Hello. This is Miss Brown. May I help you?
Hi Miss Brown. This is Jane calling.
Hi Jane.
Well I talked to the doctor and told him, you know, what we had discussed.
Yah.
He didn't say anything.
Didn't say anything at all?
No. And then I had to call him again this morning because I, you know, I've had trouble going to work everyday and he told me he thought he'd better see me Saturday.
Uh-huh.
I told him. I said I don't even know what good that does. You know. He said well he thought it was more satisfactory than a phone conversation.
So you told him this over the telephone?
Yes I did.
I see. Did you say anything about our speaking with you?
No I haven't yet.
Uh-huh. So you're supposed to see him Saturday?
Yeah.

But you don't think that that's going to be too helpful?
I don't seem to be able to cope with what I have to cope with. So I don't know what's going to happen.
What do you mean?
Well I just don't seem to be able to cope with living here, you know.
Uh-huh. Well, how has everything been going at home now?
Pretty much the same, you know. I crawl into bed early at night, right after dinner practically. And, I avoid doing what I'm supposed to do.
Uh-huh. Has your husband said anything more about your...
My husband's very upset.
Is he?
Yeah.
About you or about...
About me, mostly I guess, you know.
Uh-huh. But you don't feel that even talking and speaking with your doctor is helping too much?
No I don't.
Well how did you tell him about what we had been talking about? Do you remember what you said?
I told him I said I haven't felt anything in three months except beer.
Uh-huh. And what did he say?
He didn't say anything.
Nothing at all. Did you tell him that you've been having a hard time going to work?
Oh yes he knows that. He knows how hard it is. He told me to try to think up conversations to handle the people when I'm riding in the car but I don't know of course. I've withdrawn see so that I don't read the paper or watch t.v. or anything so I guess I don't know too much what's going on.
Uh-huh. You mean you ride with some of the people that you work with?
No. He just told me to try and think up things to say to them so that I'd have some thing to say when I got to work because you see I can't communicate with the people.
Uh-huh. I can hear laughing and people in the background there. Are they...
I'm in the Norton Union and you hear people in the hall.

I see. Uh-huh. Gee, Jane, that doesn't sound too good. I wonder how you feel... Have you been giving any thought to our calling him?
Well I just don't understand exactly how it would help.
Oh perhaps our talking to him, maybe he'd realize more, some of the things you're trying to tell him.
Well I've given thought to it but I ha... But I already have contact with him you know. I wonder what it would accomplish.
Well I wonder what you feel we would lose. Or you would lose...
I don't know. I guess I'm embarrassed that I call you every day.
And yet - if it's helping you in any kind of way... any kind of a support at all, maybe your doctor would realize that.
Well he knows that we're living pretty much as an island unto ourselves, you know. And like last night he said couldn't I have found somebody to go visit. Well there wasn't anybody. Of course I'm withdrawn so that I don't really want to see people that way when I'm so withdrawn you know and so it's like a vicious cycle.
Uh-huh. Now you said when I talked with you last that you entertained on Saturday night?
I had a couple over for cards.
Uh-huh. I wonder. When are you going to see them again? You didn't set up another time did you?
Well we're supposed to see them Saturday. He may not... they're the only ones... he knows I'm sick and she's tolerated it you know whereas the other people have just dropped us you know. Because I've been sick so much.
Well then she must be quite a good friend.
She's a nice person but I don't talk to her in between you know what I mean.
Yah. I wonder if you could try to try to confide in her.
Well maybe I should.
Maybe you should try that. That would be a good idea.
Uh-huh. Yes. Well maybe I should. Well I'll call you again Miss Brown. Ok?
That certainly is all right Jane.
Thank you.
You're welcome. Bye-Bye.

The Letter

Dear Miss Smith:

We have been here over a week, and I feel very much at home.

We moved into the house the middle of the week and worked very hard unpacking.

On Friday we went to the Beach and had a grand time.

My husband bought a small used boat last week. The motor needs some repair and we should have it for the weekend.

Thank you for all your help.

Sincerely,
Jane Black

REFERENCES

Baizerman, M.: Changing crises. *Crisis Intervention*, 6(2):45-51, 1975.
Beebe, J.: Allowing the patient to call home. *Psychother*, 5:18-20, 1968.
Bleach, G. and Claiborn, W.: Initial evaluation of hotline telephone crisis centers. *Community Ment Health J*, 10:387-394, 1974.
Brockopp, G.: The telephone call. *Crisis Int*, 2:73-75, 1970.
Brockopp, G.: An emergency telephone service. In D. Lester and G. Brockopp (Eds.): *Crisis Intervention and Counseling by Telephone.* Springfield, Thomas, 1973, pp. 9-23.
Buchta, R., Wetzel, R., Reich, T., Butler, F., and Fuller, D.: The effect of direct contact with referred crisis center clients on outcome success rates. *J Computer Psychol*, 1:395-396.
Carothers, J. and Inslee, L.: Level of empathic understanding offered by volunteer telephone services. *J Counsel Psychol*, 21:274-276, 1974.
Catanzaro, R. and Green, W.: WATS telephone therapy. *Am J Psychiatry*, 126:1024-1030, 1970.
Chiles, J.: A practical use of the telephone. *Am J Psychiatry*, 131:1030-1031.
Fowler, D. and McGee, R.: Assessing the performance of telephone crisis workers. In D. Lester and G. Brockopp (Eds): *Crisis Intervention and Counseling by Telephone.* Springfield, Thomas, 1973.
Greist, J., Gustafson, D., Strauss, F., Rowse, G., Laughren, T., and Chiles, J.: A computer interview for suicide risk prediction. *Am J Psychiatry*, 130:1327-1332, 1973.
Gruver, G.: College students as therapeutic agents. *Psychol Bull*, 76:111-127, 1971.
Hoff, L.: Beyond the telephone contact. In D. Lester and G. Brockopp (Eds): *Crisis Intervention and Counseling by Telephone.* Springfield,

Thomas, 1973.
Lamb, C.: Telephone therapy. *Voices, 5(4)*:42-46, 1970.
Lester, D.: Attempts to predict suicidal risk using psychological tests. *Psychol Bull, 74*:1-17, 1970.
Lester, D.: The chronic caller to a crisis hotline. *Crisis Intervention 3*:62-65, 1971.
Lester, D.: The evaluation of telephone counseling services. *Crisis Int, 4*:53-60, 1972.
Lester, D.: Psychologists/community crisis services. *Newsletter Division 31, 5(2)*:3, 1973.
Lester, D.: The unique qualities of telephone therapy. *Psychother, 11*:219-221, 1974. (a)
Lester, D.: Recent trends in telephone counseling. *Crisis Int, 5(2)*:8-15, 1974. (b)
Lester, D. and Brockopp, G.: *Crisis Intervention and Counseling by Telephone.* Springfield, Thomas, 1973.
MacKinnon, R. and Michels, R.: The role of the telephone in the psychiatric interview. *Psychiatry, 33*:83-93, 1970.
McColskey, A.: The use of the professional in telephone counseling. In D. Lester and G. Brockopp (Eds.): *Crisis Intervention and Counseling by Telephone.* Springfield, Thomas, 1973.
McDonough, J.: The evaluation of hotlines and crisis phone centers. *Crisis Int, 6(2)*:2-19, 1975.
McGee, R., and Jennings, B.: Ascending to "lower levels." In D. Lester and G. Brockopp (Eds): *Crisis Intervention and Counseling by Telephone.* Springfield, Thomas, 1973.
Miller, W.: The telephone in outpatient psychotherapy. *Am J Psychother, 27*:15-26, 1973.
Owens, H.: Hypnosis by phone. *Am J Clin Hypn, 13*:57-60, 1970.
Richard, W. and McGee, R.: Care team. In D. Lester and G. Brockopp (Eds): *Crisis Intervention and Counseling by Telephone.* Springfield, Thomas, 1973, pp. 149-154.
Robertiello, R.: Telephone sessions. *Psychoanal Rev, 59*:633-634, 1972.
Scheff, T.: *Being Mentally Ill.* Chicago, Aldine, 1966.
Slaikeu, K., Lester, D., and Tulkin, S.: Show versus no-show. *J Consult Clin Psychol, 40*:481-486, 1973.
Tapp, J. and Spanier, D.: Personal characteristics of volunteer phone counselors. *J Consult Clin Psychol, 41*:245-250, 1973.
Williams, T.: Telephone therapy. *Crisis Int, 3*:39-42, 1971.
Williams, T. and Dowds, J.: The unique contribution of telephone therapy. In D. Lester and G. Brockopp (Eds): *Crisis Intervention and Counseling by Telephone.* Springfield, Thomas 1973, pp. 80-88.
Wolf, A., Schwartz, E., McCarty, G., and Goldberg, I.: Training in psychoanalysis in groups without face-to-face contact. *Am J Psychother, 23*:488-494, 1969.

Chapter 3

THE USE OF THE COMPUTER IN PSYCHOTHERAPY AND COUNSELING*

IN recent years the role that computers can play in assisting the psychologist and psychiatrist has been explored, and a number of exciting possibilities have emerged. In this chapter I shall first review the major areas of application of the computer to clinical work. The advent of the computer era in clinical work has also led to concern over some of the implications of impersonalized counseling and psychotherapy. Although the issues that have been raised in this context are relevant to the use of the printed word, telephones, televisions, and tape recorders, it is only the introduction of the computer into clinical work that has made these issues sufficiently important enough that they must now be considered. I shall turn to these issues in the discussion section of this chapter.

THE COMPUTER AND CLINICAL RECORDS

The computer has been used to upgrade the quality and the character of psychological and psychiatric records and data files (Klein et al., 1975). Data on patients can be stored in a computer regarding such areas as visits, admissions, movement through the hospital or set of community agencies, medication, bills, clinical notes, and so on.

With regard to the clinical input, the notes of the clinician can be fed into the computer verbatim, or the information contained in these notes can be coded and fed in the coded format into the computer. Alternatively, a structured and standardized questionnaire can be used in place of a clinical interview. This questionnaire can contain questions pertinent to the

---
*The original version of this chapter appeared in *The Social Impact of the Telephone* published by the Massachusetts Institute of Technology Press, 1977, and is reprinted here with modifications by permission of the publisher.

patient's history and include clinical ratings of anxiety, depression, etc. or lists of symptoms. The disadvantage of the standardized questionnaire is that it is inflexible, requires dichotomous answers, and leaves little room for narrative data. (There is no reason why the individual clinician cannot also maintain a set of narrative notes for his own use.) Although the use of a questionnaire may be antithetical to the clinician's more intuitive, flexible approach to interviewing, it facilitates both research and the transfer of patients to other clinicians (since their intuitive approaches may be greatly different).

When the computer has been fed with these clinical and nonclinical records, it can easily be programmed to monitor records and warn of actions to be taken (Honigfeld, 1970). It may warn that the family physician should be notified of some event, or that a prescribed medication is inappropriate, or even that a particular patient's behavior suggests a high likelihood of some event such as elopement or suicide.

The computer can easily be programmed to take case history data fed into it in coded form and produce a narrative case history report. Klein (1970) has found that psychiatrists who have a computer-generated narrative report available to them write more inclusive case studies than psychiatrists who have available only the basic interview data.

Stroebel and Glueck (1970) included the daily nursing reports on each patient in the computerized case record and programmed the computer to print out daily charts plotting the day-to-day fluctuations in each patient's level of anxiety, depression, antisocial behavior, etc. These daily charts proved extremely useful to the staff.

Simpson (1973) applied this kind of computer application to goal setting in psychotherapy. He got each psychotherapist to list his goals with each patient and the methods of treatment that he planned to try. This information was fed into the computer and stored. The computer also generated a narrative statement of these goals and plans. At intervals during psychotherapy with each patient, the computer generates a questionnaire for the psychotherapist listing the goals he had previously established and asks him to note what progress he has made toward these goals. The computer then generates a narrative report describing the psychotherapist's progress towards his goals. The staff who utilized this system stated that they preferred this system over traditional intake and progress notes. Simpson noted that the system also helped the staff plan their treatment with each patient more fully and in a more organized fashion.

A computerized record system can be shared by a number of centers or agencies who can each update a patient's file or search the files for specific information (Gianturco and Ramm, 1971).

THE COMPUTER AND CLINICAL DECISIONS

The computer can be used to assist the clinician in making clinical decisions and can in fact make such decisions itself. Computers have been used to do the following: making clinical diagnoses; making recommendations for treatment and management of patients; prescribing the appropriate medication; referring the clinician to appropriate literature references relevant to the patient; and predicting clinical events, such as elopement risk, assaultive behavior, suicidal risk, length of stay in the hospital, effect of discharge, and response to particular treatments. Stunden (1966) has used the computer to schedule patients, student counselors, supervisors, and rooms and also to match patients with counselors based upon the skills of the counselors and the patients' requirements. The use of the computer in psychological testing will be described later in this chapter.*

The computer can be superior to the clinician in this aspect of decision making since much of the clinician's knowledge can be programmed into the computer (see Kleinmuntz, 1963, for an example of this) and since the computer can use more complex decision-making rules than a human and make the decisions faster. For example, computers can utilize Bayes theorem, cluster analysis, pattern recognition, factor analysis, and

---

*Obviously, computers can also be used to improve prediction by generating useful formula, such as step-wise linear discriminant functions that the clinician then applies (for example, Lester et al. [1975] for the prediction of homicide or Mendels [1967] for the prediction of response to ECT).

regression analysis.

The data from which the computer generates these clinical decisions can be fed into the computer in various formats. Obviously, it is easier if the data are fed into the computer in a standardized format. Spitzer and Endicott (1969) have described a program that generates a psychiatric diagnosis from structured input from a response sheet completed by the interviewing psychiatrist. Benfari et al. (1972), however, have programmed a computer to take in a narrative case report, pick out key words (such as anxiety, skin, guilt, etc.), and generate a diagnosis from these data.

The computer can also accept data directly from the patient as shall be discussed next.

INTAKE INTERVIEW BY COMPUTER

A patient (or relative of the patient) can complete an interview by directly responding to computer-readable questionnaire or he can directly type responses into a computer in response to computer-generated questions. Most patients can be easily taught to use a computer terminal, and the computer generated interview can follow quite closely the human-directed interview.

A computer-generated interview has several advantages. The data collected are complete, standardized (in the setting of the interview, the wording of the questions, the sequence of questions, the inter-question time period, etc.), legible, accurate, and already stored, and have an easily available summary. A computer-generated interview saves the clinician time in the collection and reporting of intake data.

The computer generated interview also eliminates experimenter variables. The computer can be programmed to be impersonal and nonjudgmental. It is objective and can be conceptually neutral. The interview can also be flexible; it can be programmed to branch, that is, to go in different directions depending upon the particular answers that the patient gives.

The reports generated by the computer are more efficient, retain all of the information, use meaningful terminology, have an acceptable format and size, and improve both the communication and education of the staff. (Obviously, for this to be the case, the person who initially programs the computer must work closely with skilled staff members.)

A computer-generated interview also is available at any time of the day or night and proceeds at the pace that the patient desires. A computer generated interview also gives the patient a greater feeling of control over what is taking place than a face-to-face interview does. A computer-generated interview can have rest periods built into it and humor too.

A computer generated interview is also economical. The cost of an interview to predict suicidal risk devised by Greist et al. (1973) took an average of eighty-two minutes for the patient to complete and cost $4.25 during weekdays.

Patients find computer interviews acceptable. Coddington and King (1972) had the mothers of children who were in treatment respond to a computer interview concerning the symptomatology of their children. Fifty percent reported the computer interview to be easier than a face-to-face discussion with the doctor, whereas only 37 percent found it to be more difficult. Sixty-seven percent reported that they were as frank with the computer as in face-to-face interviews, and 15 percent reported that they were more frank.

Greist et al. (1973) devised an interview based upon the clinical intuition and knowledge of eight psychiatrists that would predict suicidal risk. Fifty-two percent of the patients given the interview preferred the computer mode (as compared to 27 percent of patients given an interview about symptoms). The computer prediction of attempted suicide was more accurate than a clinician's prediction based on the same data. Greist suggested that it may be easier to divulge socially deviant behavior to a nonjudgmental interviewer than to a human directly.

Greist et al. also noted that all of the patients completed the interview and that some (especially those who took the longest time) seemed less disturbed after the interview. The interview appeared to have, therefore, an ego-orienting effect.

Slack (1971) described a computer-interviewing system that also monitored heart rate and keyboard response times. The computer was programmed to respond to the direct keyboard responses and to these nonverbal measures. For example, if the patient's heart rate increased the computer would respond with "Relax, you're doing fine" and report this information to the experimenter. The program would also change the topic if the patient appeared too anxious. Slack noted that this system obtains information from the patient without the patient having control over it, since the autonomic nervous system is outside of conscious control. (The patient obviously agrees to the attachment of the appropriate monitors.) Thus, Slack's system raises important ethical issues as to whether indirect or covert monitoring of patients should be permitted.

THE COMPUTER AND CLINICAL EDUCATION

The computer can be programmed to present a student with simulated cases. The student must decide upon the questions to be asked, the areas to be explored, and the tests to be ordered. He can also be asked to suggest appropriate treatments. The program can provide feedback on the accuracy of the student's diagnosis, the probable success of treatment, and mistakes made by the student. Friedman (1973) has described a program that accomplishes this aim for medical students and which incorporates a cost factor (it prices the various tests ordered by the student) and a time factor (eventually the patient dies).

These programs need not simulate the actual dialogue between patient and clinician. They can present questions to the student, such as "Which test do you want to order next?" and have him respond to these questions. Other programs exist which simulate patient-clinician dialogue, and these too can be used for training students of psychotherapy. These simulated dialogue programs will be discussed later in this chapter.

THE COMPUTER AND MENTAL HEALTH PLANNING

The computer can also be used in planning mental health services via the design of computer simulation models. For example, the effect of expanding a service with nurses as opposed to psychiatrists can be explored using a computer simulation model. The best investment of money can be compared with the most efficient service and a compromise worked out (Pearce, 1967).

THE COMPUTER AND PSYCHOLOGICAL TESTING

Some psychological tests, such as the MMPI, Ravens Progressive Matrices, and some subtests of the Wechsler Adult Intelligence Scale can be administered by a computer. As in the computer-generated intake interviews described above, this results in standardized, objective, and error-free testing with elimination of clinician variables. The scoring is also immediate. Dunn et al. (1972) claimed that patients may be more open and honest with a computer-administered test.

Evan and Miller (1969) found that students responding to the Lie Scale of the MMPI lied less when the scale was administered by computer than when they filled out the questionnaire alone and signed their names to it. They did not find any differences in acquiescence responses or belief in whether their data would be confidential. (Evan and Miller noted, however, that their computer-administered groups and control groups differed in experience of computer courses!)

Koson et al. (1970) found no differences in defensiveness using the K Scale of the MMPI and embarrassing and threatening questions administered by computer with experimenter absent, administered in a paper and pencil format in the presence of the experimenter or read aloud by the experimenter who also recorded the subject's responses.

Paitich (1973) has described a computer-administered battery of tests, complete with automated scoring and computer-generated report. Knights and Watson (1968) have described how the computer can be used to take a profile from a battery of tests and generate matching profiles from a store of profiles of patients with known disorders and prognoses.

Some resistance and anxiety is found in some subjects who take computer-administered psychological tests, but this is often a result of poor programming. For example the program may not permit a subject to correct a wrong answer (Dunn et al., 1972), or it may keep asking more and more difficult questions even after the subject has failed three consecutive items (Hedl et al., 1973).

COMPUTER INTERPRETATION OF PSYCHOLOGICAL TESTS

The computer has also been used in the interpretation of psychological tests. Computer interpretation has been used primarily with the MMPI, but it has also been applied to other psychological tests, such as the Rorschach (Piotrowski, 1964) and the TAT (Smith, 1968) who used the General Inquirer System of content analysis (Stone, et al., 1967) to score for n-ach, n-aff and n-pow.

Returning to the MMPI, a system of computer interpretation can be based upon clinical information fed into the computer. For example, Fowler (1968) has used nonacturial information, that is, his clinical interpretations of various MMPI profiles and signs, in order to provide an interpretation, and he has supplemented this with research findings. Marks and Seeman (1963), on the other hand, have used primarily actuarial, research-generated data as the basis for a computer interpretation.

Kleinmuntz (1963) has illustrated a variant of computer-based MMPI interpretation using clinical judgment. Kleinmuntz selected the best MMPI interpreter that he could find and had him sort hundreds of MMPI protocols into maladjusted and adjusted piles, while verbalizing his criteria out loud. Kleinmuntz then took the hours of verbalization made by the clinician and reduced them to objective rules that could be programmed for computer use. Kleinmuntz then compared the accuracy of the clinician and the computer program in classifying college students by matching their judgments with those of the student's counselors. The computer program was more accurate than the clinician, even though it was using his rules. Clearly, the computer was able to apply the rules more consistently and uniformly and was able to deal better with rules that gave conflicting decisions. Kleinmuntz tried to improve the computer program by adding rules derived from research data and the hit rate improved still further. It was also easier to introduce moderator variables using the computer program. In a follow-up study on the program, the computer program was found to be as good as the best clinician and better than the average clinician (Kleinmuntz, 1967). (Fowler et al., 1968, however, found that Kleinmuntz's Mt scale was a more accurate predictor of counselor's ratings of maladjustment in college students than was the computer program derived by Kleinmuntz.)

How good are computer interpretations of the MMPI? Webb et al. (1970) had clinicians rate Fowler's computer-derived and clinically-derived MMPI interpretations.Twenty-two percent felt that the computer interpretation was worse, 39 percent felt that it was as good, and 40 percent felt that it was better. Bringmann et al. (1972) compared a simple computer-derived interpretation (based on clinical intuition) with interpretations prepared by graduate students. The computer-derived interpretations were rated better than student-derived interpretations for elevated profiles but worse for normal profiles. Bringmann, however, did not use one of the major computer-derived interpreting systems and so his study is by no means an adequate test of computer interpretations.

THE COMPUTER AND BEHAVIOR THERAPY

It has been noted by many behavior therapists that the techniques of behavior therapy can be automated quite easily. It is easy to arrange for a computer to carry out systematic desensitization, for example, and such automation has the advantage that physiological data from the patient can be fed into the computer and help determine the course of the therapy.

Automated desensitization using a computer has been found to be as effective as a human therapist in treating test anxiety (Donner and Guerney, 1969). In addition, since the cure rate with human behavior therapists is directly related to the time spent by the therapist on the desensitization (Eysenck and Rachman, 1965), Stodolsky (1970) has argued that computer-administered desensitization should lead to a higher cure rate since the computer can allow patients to spend larger amounts of time interacting with the program than they could spend interacting with a human therapist.

Computers have also been found useful in shaping behaviors such as speech responses. Colby (1973), for example, noted that autistic children have as their primary difficulty an inability to process symbols. He noted that the prognosis of autistic children was correlated with their ability to speak and that autistic children play more willingly with machines than with humans. All this suggested that autistic children could be helped by computer-administered speech games. The child, for example, pushes a key and a symbol may appear on a screen or a sound may be emitted. If a child presses the "H" key, a letter "H" may appear on the screen, there may be a sound of horses hooves and a picture of a horse, or a human voice may say "H." The child controls the machine, which never tires and never gets angry or bored. The machine is predictable, consistent, and controlled. Colby employed a human sitter who encouraged the children but did not participate any more than that. Of seventeen autistic children who were used, thirteen showed an improvement in their speech.

PRE-TESTING PSYCHOTHERAPY WITH A COMPUTER

Loehlin (1968) proposed that a psychotherapist considering a drastic psychotherapeutic intervention with a patient might first try the intervention out on a computer model of the patient. If the model responds unfavorably to the intervention, then the psychotherapist might want to think twice before trying it on the patient.

Loehlin noted that no one had yet constructed a computer model of a human personality that was of any use except as an interesting artifact in itself or as a portent of things to come. However, the shape of things to come can be illustrated.

Loehlin constructed a simple computer-simulated personality, whom he called *Aldous*. For *Aldous* to operate, some stimulus, such as "a dark-haired male adult," is fed into the computer. *Aldous* has a memory — a record of his emotional reaction to dark-haired people, to males, to adults, to male adults, and so on. Three emotions were programmed: fear, anger, and love. The emotional reaction to a stimulus is determined both by *Aldous's* past experience with stimuli and by his current mood. The emotions generated by the stimulus are stored and an action selected such as: withdrawal, attack, approach, paralysis, and no reaction.

In one experiment two *Aldouses* were put into the computer. One had a set of positive initial attitudes and the other had a set of negative initial attitudes. Both *Aldouses* ended the series of interactions with mutual hostility. Psychotherapy was then tried.

Aldous A was made to be totally benevolent. He gave a positive output for any input. *Aldous B* became violently aggressive. Then *Aldous A* was programmed as follows:

B's withdrawal was met by mild positive approach by A.
Mild aggression was met with strong aggression.
Strong aggression was met with mild withdrawal.
Neutral, positive or ambivalent actions were met with a strong positive response.

Eventually *Aldous B* developed strongly positive attitudes and behavior. When *Aldous B* was put back with his original partner quarrels developed, and *Aldous B* became more negative in attitude and behavior. He was returned to *Aldous A* (his therapist) and after treatment formed a stable positive relationship with his original partner.

This illustrates how various psychotherapeutic strategies may be tried out on a patient in computer simulation. Of course, the particular patient models developed by Loehlin are of limited use to practicing psychotherapists.

COMPUTER-GENERATED DIALOGUES IN TRAINING CLINICIANS

Loehlin (1968) suggested that psychotherapists could train using computer models of patients. A computer model would provide dependable practice cases that have known properties and would spare patients the wear and tear of having neophyte psychotherapists. Loehlin suggested the use of artifical textbooks cases or realistic cases that presented the trainee with a range of situations with which he has to deal. The program could present alternative solutions or, as shall be seen below, actual dialogue. In this way, the same patient at different stages of psychotherapy could be presented to a trainee, or alternatively, the onset of sudden panic could be studied in slow motion.

The best example of a computer program that could be used for training psychotherapists is that devised by Colby (1975) who had written a program that simulates the conversation of a paranoidal person. The computer responds to input that is typed into a teletype in natural language, and it responds in natural language. The level of fear, anger, and mistrust of the paranoidal model can be varied and the program made to simulate strong or weak paranoia. The extract of conversation below comes from the program in its weak form. Sentences labelled "I" are produced by the human, those labelled "O" by the program.

(1) I--How long have you been in the hospital?
O--About a week.
(2) I--Are You depressed?
O--No.
(3) I--Were you taking drugs?
O--No.
(4) I--What is your problem?
O--People make me nervous.
(5) I--How do they do that?
O--They stare at me.
(6) I--Why?
O--Maybe they don't like the way I look or something.
(7) I--Do you look unusual in some way?
O--Why are you interested in my looks?
(8) I--Because you said people stare at you.
O--Well, sometimes.
(9) I--How do you get along with people?
O--I don't communicate very much with others.
(10) I--Why not?
O--They don't realize what's going on most of the time.
(11) I--What is going on?

O--Do you know how the underworld operates?
(From Colby et al., 1971, p. 323)

A group of psychiatrists were asked to interview a real patient and the program via a teletype and were not able to distinguish the real patient from the computer program (neither could computer scientists). Colby noted that his model can be used to explore theories of paranoia and to investigate how psychiatric judgments are made. For training purposes, the trainees can practice with the program alone or with a supervisor and they can also have transcripts of their interviewers easily made as they work with the program. Such a model can also be adapted to form a standardized test of psychotherapeutic skills.

THE COMPUTER AS A PSYCHOTHERAPIST

A number of writers have noted that there is a shortage of psychotherapists today. If computer programs could be devised that could simulate psychotherapeutic behavior, more people could have cheap and easy access to psychotherapy. For research purposes, computer-simulated psychotherapy would give the experimenter greater control over extraneous variables (Stodolsky, 1970).

A computer program functioning psychotherapeutically could be programmed to give a standard pattern of responses, to engage in a nondirective dialogue, to engage in a quasi-social interaction with the patient, or to be a problem-solving experience suggesting different alternatives to particular problems posed by the patient.

The best example of a nondirective psychotherapeutic program is that of *Eliza* (or *Doctor*) devised by Weizenbaum (1966). The human is asked to put himself in a role-playing frame of mind in which he is to imagine that he has some problem of the kind he might choose to discuss with a psychotherapist. He is to pretend that he is talking to a psychotherapist, and he is not to deviate from that role. (As soon as the person leaves this role, the quality of the responses produced by the program deteriorates.)

The program is nondirective and restricts itself to pointing out new connective opportunities to the person. The hope could be, if the program were utilized as a psychotherapist, that the reorganization of the patient's ideas will reflect itself in a corresponding modification of his belief systems and thence his behavior.

The program does more. Weizenbaum reported an anecdote in which his secretary asked to use the program. After typing in a few responses, she asked Weizenbaum to leave the room. Weizenbaum noted that the program creates an illusion of understanding and that there is some rapport established between the human and the program. The following is typical conversation between a human and the Rogerian form of *Eliza*. The capitalized lines are those generated by the computer program.)

Men are all alike.
IN WHAT WAY?
They're always bugging us about something or other.
CAN YOU THINK OF A SPECIFIC EXAMPLE
Well, my boyfriend made me come here.
YOUR BOYFRIEND MADE YOU COME HERE
He says I'm depressed much of the time.
I AM SORRY TO HEAR YOU ARE DEPRESSED
It's true. I am unhappy.
DO YOU THINK COMING HERE WILL HELP YOU NOT TO BE UNHAPPY
I need some help, that much seems certain.
WHAT WOULD IT MEAN TO YOU IF YOU GOT SOME HELP
Perhaps I could learn to get along with my mother.
TELL ME MORE ABOUT YOUR FAMILY
My mother takes care of me.
WHO ELSE IN YOUR FAMILY TAKES CARE OF YOU
My father.
YOUR FATHER
You are like my father in some ways.
WHAT RESEMBLANCE DO YOU SEE
You are not very aggressive but I think you don't want me to notice that.
WHAT MAKES YOU THINK I AM NOT VERY AGGRESSIVE

You don't argue with me.
WHY DO YOU THINK I DON'T ARGUE WITH YOU
You are afraid of me.
DOES IT PLEASE YOU TO BELIEVE I AM AFRAID OF YOU
My father is afraid of everybody.
WHAT ELSE COMES TO MIND WHEN YOU THINK OF YOUR FATHER
Bullies.
DOES THAT HAVE ANYTHING TO DO WITH THE FACT THAT YOUR BOYFRIEND MADE YOU COME HERE
(From Weizenbaum, 1966, pp. 36-37)

Colby and Enea (1967) noted that these early programs had many weak points. They often lost the thread of what was being said and so gave an inappropriate response. They often responded to a trivial part of a patient's input. They also failed to store information about the patient and so would ask for example about a relative whom the patient had already described as dead. These problems may eventually be eliminated.

Despite the faults of these early programs, they were surprisingly successful in creating the illusion of a psychotherapist. McGuire et al. (1967) asked users of *Eliza* about their experience with *Eliza* and 62 percent thought that they were or probably were conversing with a human, even though the computer program often generated inappropriate responses. The users "forgave" these responses much as they might with fellow humans. Many of the users believed that they were being "understood."

Hilf (1972) felt that present computer programs for conducting conversations and psychotherapy with patients were too inadequate to be really useful. Patients have varied vocabularies and dialects. They often use unconventional expressions and neologisms. Computer programs currently in use cannot cope with this variation.

Hilf, for demonstration purposes, tried a variant of the computer-patient interaction. He utilized a computer program for conversing with the patient, and he limited the function of the program to diagnosis. So, the computer asked questions relevant only to deciding upon a diagnosis. However, Hilf introduced into the system a human translator. When the patient typed a response, the human read the response and translated it into terms that the computer could understand unambiguously. The translator typed the translated response directly into the computer. (The patient was not aware of the translator's presence.) Obviously, such a system is no more efficient than using the human to ask questions directly (either face-to-face or via a teletype). To be useful, a way has to be found of programming a computer to function as a translator. Some sample interviews generated by this method are shown below. (The capitalized lines are those generated by the computer program.)

#1)
HELLO, MY NAME IS DOCTOR ERNEST, WHAT IS YOURS
Betty Jones, but my real name is Sarah Peters.
HOW OLD ARE YOU
Twenty-nine
ARE YOU MARRIED
Yes.....
... DO YOU HAVE TROUBLE SLEEPING
Yes
DO YOU FIND IT DIFFICULT TO FALL ASLEEP
Yes
DO YOU WAKE UP AFTER HAVING SLEPT ONLY A FEW HOURS AND THEN CAN'T FALL BACK TO SLEEP
I don't do that too often
DO YOU TAKE SLEEPING PILLS
Only when I try to kill myself.....
#2)
HELLO, MY NAME IS DOCTOR ERNEST, WHAT IS YOURS
6940263900
PLEASE TYPE IN YOUR NAME OTHERWISE WE CAN'T CONTINUE
Johnny Ward
JOHNNY, ARE YOU A MAN OR WOMAN
Strike up the band.
WHAT IS YOUR SEX

Neuter.
HOW OLD ARE YOU, JOHNNY
Centuries.
WHAT IS YOUR MARITAL STATUS
Married to Almighty God.
(From Hilf, 1972, pp. 416-417)

Colby, et al. (1966) have pointed out that eventually computer programs for counseling will require much greater complexity than current programs. It would be useful, for example to have different programs for the different stages of psychotherapy. Current programs model only the initial stages of psychotherapy and we obviously need programs to conduct the middle and final stages. It would also be useful if the programs could build up a cognitive model of the client and base its responses to the client upon this cognitive model. In this way, the computer's responses would be more tailored to the individual needs of each client.

THE COMPUTER IN VOCATIONAL GUIDANCE

Vocational guidance is particularly well suited to the inclusion of computer-based services. Vocational guidance involves a good deal of information giving, for the client is often uninformed about the varied possibilities for his career and the kinds of tasks that different careers will involve. This transmission of information can, of course, be achieved by giving the client books and pamphlets to read. However, the information can also be stored in computers and presented to the client while he is seated at a computer terminal.

In addition, vocational guidance relies much more than psychotherapy upon information obtained from the client in the form of aptitude and interest surveys. Although, of course, psychotherapists can and do administer psychological tests to their clients, the majority do not. For example, Meehl (1972) reported that only 17 percent of psychotherapists who were surveyed felt that psychological test data (mainly the Rorschach and the TAT) greatly speeded the course of psychotherapy. The vocational guidance counselor finds psychological test data extremely useful. The information from these tests can easily be stored in the computer and then used either to select the particular information that will be displayed to the client or to match the career choices being considered by the client against his interests and abilities.

Chick (1970) has reviewed existing computer-based vocational guidance systems. Most of these systems are directed toward supplementing the role of the counselor rather than replacing the vocational counselor. The systems facilitate the transmission of information to the client and facilitate the education of the client in vocational choices. This means that face-to-face contacts between the client and the vocational counselor can be spent in more profitable activities.

An illustration of a computer-based vocational guidance system will indicate the potential usefulness of such systems. The Information System for Vocational Decisions (Tiedman, 1966) is designed to help clients connect information about themselves with information about education, training, and work. The system is designed to provide clients with information on which the clients can base their vocational decisions. The computer is programmed to provide information readily and in a useable form when needed. The vocational counselor can then function solely as an interpreter rather than as a provider of information. The ISVD system has three basic files, with information on educational, military, and vocational opportunities. Each file is subdivided into exploratory and clarification stages, with fewer and more general facts being presented in the former stage than in the latter stage.

The client interacts with the computer through a teletype outlet connected to a visual display. The computer interacts with the client by means of a free-flowing intelligible conversation, and a record of this interaction is stored in the computer. Other systems can provide a written record of the interaction for the client to keep for review or for discussion with his vocational counselor (or his parents, etc.). The visual display is used to show slides with an accompanying tape recording describing what is being shown on the slides and providing other related information.

The ISVD system has teaching scripts that teach the client facts related to career choice, preference scripts designed to help the client transform vague preferences about criteria for work or school into concrete alternatives which are then displayed for the client and stored in the computer, data retrieval scripts which permit the client to ask for specific information about careers and schools, and game scripts in which the client can make educational and vocational plans for a hypothetical person described to him by the computer.

At certain points in an interaction with the computer, the computer may encourage the client to see his vocational counselor. This happens, for example, when the client continues to explore an occupation that seems incompatible with his abilities and interests. The vocational counselor's role is therefore to provide professional counseling and to help the client use the facts and data provided through the computer-based informational system.

Computer-based vocational guidance systems can also provide information to the vocational counselor in the same way as the system does for the client. The vocational counselor can have a computer outlet in his office which can then be used to retrieve information on educational and career opportunities. The computer can also be used to store personal data on the vocational counselor's clients, such as their vocational interests and aptitudes, their educational record, etc. (Minor et al., 1969).

Other computer-based vocational guidance systems have been devised by Harris (1968), Katz (1969), Impellitteri (1969), Loughary, et al. (1966), and Youst (1969).

Advantages For The Client

Chick (1970) reviewed the advantages of computer-based vocational guidance systems for the client and noted the following.

(1) The information provided is accurate, current, organized, and more extensive than most vocational counselors can provide.
(2) The information is presented in an unbiased way without

value judgements.
(3) The computer's memory and recall is infallible.
(4) The client can receive a print-out of the interaction for his later personal review or for discussions with the vocational counselor. He is less likely to forget the information he was given.
(5) Clients feel a greater sense of involvement and personal responsibility in determining their future plans. They have to initiate the contact, maintain attention, and control the computer (the speed of progress, the number of reviews, the directions explored, etc.).
(6) It has been found that clients sometimes find it easier to tell a computer their desires and plans than to tell another person. The computer is safe, for it does not judge their plans. It does not communicate nonverbally by the tone of voice or a raised eyebrow. Interacting with the computer is often fun (Youst, 1969) and so can motivate the client to use vocational material.
(7) Access to the information in the computer is often easier than seeking out the vocational counselor, particularly if the client-counselor ratio is high.
(8) The face-to-face counseling sessions are more productive since the clients are better informed. The level of intellectual exchange and level of problem solving are much higher with more informed clients.
(9) Computer-based systems can include predictive data to help the client evaluate his chances of success against normative groups.

Advantages For The Counselor

(1) A computer-based vocational counseling system can free the vocational counselor from having to perform the mechanical tasks of data transmission, storage, and retrieval. He can thus devote more time to counseling. (Of course, someone has to be employed updating and programming the computer!) The counselor can also reach and service larger numbers of clients.

(2) Computer-based information can be updated more easily than printed documents and the computer can manage and process the vast amounts of information available in educational and vocational areas.
(3) Counselors can use the system to retrieve information on careers for their own use in counseling, or to get a review of which clients used the system and what kinds of interests the clients were pursuing. (This latter use raises ethical issues as to the conditions under which the counselor has this right. Some clients may prefer confidentiality for their interactions with the computer, and they could easily be permitted this privilege.) The computer can be programmed to alert the counselor to any discrepancies or problems with a client that require a counselor's intervention or advice.
(4) Client records can be retrieved quickly and without effort.
(5) The print-out of computer-client interactions can be useful in face-to-face discussions with the client.

Disadvantages

(1) Computer-based systems require considerable expenditure of time, money, and personnel. Maintenance of the system is cheaper than setting it up but can still be prohibitively expensive for some institutions.
(2) Computer-based approaches may not be suitable for all clients. Other alternatives (such as printed materials) must be available for those who cannot use or choose not to use a computer-based system. Melhus et al. (1973) gave high school students the Educational Development Series Tests and obtained a group of high scorers and a group of low scorers. Each group was divided into two subgroups who received either computerized vocational guidance counseling (Harris, 1968) or face-to-face counseling. The groups did not differ in their satisfaction with the advice they received. The group with high scores on the readiness tests also showed no differences in the amount of change in their career plans as a result of

receiving one kind of counseling versus the other. In contrast the low readiness students changed their career plans more after the face-to-face counseling than after the computer counseling. (However, Melhus et al. presented no evidence to indicate whether the change was for the better or not.) This study supports the notion (Hershenson, 1969) that different vocational counseling methods may be differentially effective for clients of differing readiness or maturity.

Conclusions

Computer-based vocational information systems have not been designed to replace vocational counselors. They have been designed to supplement the services of the vocational counselor and to free him from the more mechanical aspects of his task. However, the use of computer-based systems will change the vocational counselor's role and, though many will welcome this change, some may not. In a time of a shortage of trained personnel for effective counseling of all the people who could benefit from such counseling, the freeing of a counselor's time from tasks that can be done more efficiently by a mechanical device is clearly welcome.

EDUCATION AS COUNSELING

Cassel (1971; Cassel and Blum, 1969) has argued that people will make better choices about life decisions if they are better informed. Consequently, he has designed computerized quizzes in which the student is presented with a hypothetical life situation and asked to choose the correct choice from a number of alternatives. The correct choice is always that answer that agrees most with the values of the society. The student is given feedback as to the correctness of his choice. Cassel has used this approach to educate school children about drug abuse, that is, to teach them the choices that society wants from them, and to try to get the values of delinquents more in line with those of the society. Cassel has not yet reported any data that evaluates the success of this indirect approach to counseling.

CRITICISMS OF COMPUTER APPLICATIONS

Many criticisms have been made of computer applications in counseling. Some of the older criticisms are now invalid. For example, Holtzman (1960) argued that computer services were uneconomical and could not match the clinician's thought processes. As reported above, Greist et al. (1973) calculated that an interview to predict suicidal risk, lasting an average of eighty-two minutes, cost only $4.25. The establishment of a computerized system is costly, but through time-sharing, large numbers of users can tap into one system and make the operation of the system quite economical. The work of Kleinmuntz (1963), also reported above, showed that he was able to write a computer program based upon a clinician's thought processes and that it actually performed better than by the clinician on subsequent tests.

Holtzman (1960) also argued that the computer-client interaction was impersonal. Weizenbaum (1976) has argued similarly. Weizenbaum discussed computer-based nondirective psychotherapy and reported that people became emotionally involved with the computer. They anthropomorphized it. For example, Weizenbaum's secretary, after a few exchanges with the computer program, asked him to leave the room. When he proposed monitoring all conversations with the program, people objected to his monitoring other people's intimate thoughts. According to Weizenbaum, then, short exposure to a computer program can evidently induce powerful delusional thinking in normal people. People were conversing with a computer as if it were a person who could be appropriate and usefully addressed in intimate terms.

Weizenbaum argued that to use a computer as a psychotherapist is feasible but immoral. People may get help from interacting with a computer even though it does not understand them, but they think that the computer does understand them. It is a fraud and a charlatanism. Some human functions ought not to have computers substituted. The ability of the computer to perform the function has nothing to do with it. Respect, understanding, and love are crucial components in some human functions and the computer cannot provide these.

Weizenbaum's objections are somewhat emotional. First, his anecdotal data seems to contradict Holtzman's fear that computer counseling is too impersonal. Weizenbaum feels that it can become too personal!

Secondly, there is fraud only if the clients are not informed about the system. If they are not told that a computer program generates the replies, they may well assume that there is a person somewhere in the system, listening to their input and understanding them. The computer system is not fraudulent, only the people who manage the system.

Thirdly, ethics are subjective. It might be considered unethical to withhold a treatment modality that might benefit people who would use it, were it available.

Colby (1967) has addressed this issue cogently. Computer programs are devised by men, and so they can reflect any values that those men choose to program into them. Thus, computers do have a human element. Secondly, Colby noted that if you think computers are impersonal and dehumanizing, then you should visit your local state psychiatric hospital, where people are herded into wards with virtually no contact with psychotherapists. In such understaffed, virtually custodial institutions, any psychotherapeutic input is valuable. And what if the computer program outperformed some (or even most) clinicians? Finally, I would add, by way of an example, that no computer has yet sexually seduced its client, unlike many psychotherapists.

The use of computer-based systems has also led some to express concern with the confidentiality of the client's input to the computer. In fact, computer-based systems can be made much more secure than paper-and-pencil files if the necessary arrangements are built into the system. I have visited clinics, on the other hand, where patient files were open to all of the professional staff, the secretaries, and some seventy volunteer nonprofessional telephone counselors. The use of computer-based systems has certainly stimulated the discussion of confidentiality, but it certainly has not created the problem.

A common criticism of computer-based systems is that they usurp the counselor's role. It is common for professionals to seek to establish and fortify their professional jurisdiction and to feel threatened when their roles are changed. This state of affairs suggests a need for counseling for professionals rather than abandoning the use of effective counseling aids.

Loehlin (1968) has warned that computers may be able to change beliefs and attitudes, that is to say, indoctrinate people. Again, computers have no dominance here. Halleck (1971) has warned of the same danger in face-to-face psychotherapy, where in fact the danger is much greater.

Finally, Loehlin has noted that in the use of computer-based systems there is a diffusion of responsibility for action and decision. If a blunder is made, for example, whom do you sue? — the program writer, the computer operator or the psychiatrist who sent you to the computer? There are obvious legal issues involved here that, as yet, remain unresolved.

DISCUSSION

In Chapter 6, there will be a detailed discussion of the implications of the use of communications technology in counseling. A few thoughts, however, are pertinent here.

Weizenbaum (1966) noted that his aim in constructing Eliza was not to produce a computer program that would conduct psychotherapy. His aim was to explore programs that would enable a study to be made of natural language communication between man and computer. Why did he choose a psychiatric interview, based on Rogerian technique for his initial attempt?

> From the purely technical point of view then, the psychiatric interview form on an *Eliza* script has the advantage that it eliminates the need of storing *explicit* information about the real world. (Weizenbaum, 1966, p. 42)

This means that a program that simulates a Rogerian psychotherapist need have no explicit information about the real world (or to be accurate, very little information). Does this imply that a Rogerian psychotherapist need have no explicit information about the real world? By analogy, it would seem to. For example, if you tell your psychotherapist "I went for a ride in a boat" and he replies "Tell me more about boats," you do not assume that he knows nothing about boats. You assume that he has some purpose in directing the conversation in that direction.

Does this explain why nonprofessionals and paraprofessionals, who do not have even a high school education, can sometimes perform effectively as counselors? Or why psychiatric patients can have psychotherapeutic effects on other patients?

Furthermore, the work reviewed above leads to the question of whether the psychotherapist's presence is necessary or even useful. Patients may act more disturbed than they actually are in order to enlist the sympathy of the psychotherapist. In self-mutilation behavior, removal of the psychotherapist often reduces the rate of self-destructive behavior (Lovaas and Simmons, 1968).

Perhaps we should assume that psychotherapists do have some intrinsic value, but there are few data on how they compare with computers. Some of the data cited in this chapter indicate that computers can compete favorably with human psychotherapists (see Smith, 1963; Greist et al., 1973). People given problems to solve do better if the problems are administered by a computer and their performances have less variability (Smith, 1963). Subjects reported less frustration and more encouragement from the computer-administered problems. On personal questions, some people respond more honestly and with more candor even though they know their answers would later be scrutinized by a human (Evan and Miller, 1969; Slack and Van Cura, 1968).

One noteworthy possibility for computer-based interviewing is the potential for taking both verbal and physiological input from the client and moderating the responses to the client in the light of both sets of information. A computer-based system may be much more able to do this than a human counselor.

And finally, it should be noted that computer-client interactions permit the client to experience and have much more power than he would have in face-to-face counseling. As noted in Chapter 2 on counseling by telephone, this power may facilitate psychotherapeutic movement in the client.

Some of these issues will be returned to in greater detail in the final chapter of this book.

REFERENCES

Benfari, R., Leighton, A., Beiser, M., and Coen, K.: Case. *J Nerv Ment Dis,* *154*:115-124, 1972.

Bringmann, W., Balance, W., and Giesbrecht, C.: The computer versus the technologist. *Psychol Rep, 31*:211-217, 1972.

Cassel, R.: Systems analysis approach to computer-based counseling for addiction treatment. *Int J Addict, 6*:493-495, 1971.

Cassel, R. and Blum, L.: Computer-assisted counseling for the prevention of delinquent behavior among teenagers and youth. *Sociol Social Res, 54*:72-79, 1969.

Chick, J.: *Innovations in the Use of Career Information.* Boston, H-M, 1970.

Coddington, R. and King, T.: Automated history taking in child psychiatry. *Am J Psychiatry, 129*:276-282, 1972.

Colby, K.: Computer simulation of change in personal belief systems. *Behav Sci, 12*:248-253, 1967.

Colby, K.: The rationale for computer-based treatment of language difficulties in nonspeaking autistic children. *J Autism Child Schizo, 3*:254-260, 1973.

Colby, K.: *Artificial Paranoia.* New York, Pergamon, 1975.

Colby, K. and Enea, H.: Heuristic methods for computer understanding of natural language in context-restricted on-line dialogues. *Math Biosci, 1*:1-25, 1967.

Colby, K., Watt, J., and Gilbert, J.: A computer method of psychotherapy. *J Nerv Ment Dis., 142*:148-152, 1966.

Colby, K., Weber, S., and Hilf, F.: Artificial paranoia. *Artifical Int, 2*:1-25, 1971.

Donner, L., and Guerney, B.: Automated group desensitization for test anxiety. *Behav Res Ther, 7*:1-13, 1969.

Dunn, T., Lushene, R., and O'Neil, H.: Complete automation of the MMPI and a study of its response latencies. *J Consult Clin Psychol, 39*:381-387, 1972.

Evan, W. and Miller, J.: Differential effects of response bias of computer versus conventional administration of a social science questionnaire. *Behav Sci, 14*:216-227, 1969.

Eysenck, H. and Rachman, S.: *The Causes and Cures of Neurosis.* London, Knapp, 1965.

Fowler, R.: MMPI computer interpretation for college counseling. *J Psychol, 69*:201-207, 1968.

Fowler, R., Stevens, S., Coyle, F., and Marlowe, G.: Comparison of two methods of identifying maladjusted college students. *J Psychol, 69*:165-168, 1968.

Friedman, R.: A computer-based program for simulating the patient-physician encounter. *J Med Educ, 48*:92-97, 1973.

Gianturco, D., and Ramm, D.: A conversational psychiatric information network. *Community Ment Health J, 7*:127-133, 1971.

Greist, J., Gustafson, D., Strauss, F., Rowse, G., Laughren, T., and Chiles, J.: A computer interview for suicide risk prediction. *Am J Psychiatry, 130*:1327-1332, 1973.

Halleck, S.: *The Politics of Therapy.* New York Science House, 1971.

Harris, J.: The computerization of vocational information. *Vocat Guid Quart, 17*:12-20, 1968.

Hedl, J., O'Neil, H., and Hansen, D.: Affective reactions toward computer-based intelligence testing. *J Consult Clin Psychol, 40*:217-222, 1973.

Hershenson, D.: Techniques for assisting life-stage vocational development. *Pers Guid J, 47*:776-780, 1969.

Hilf, F.: Partially automated psychiatric interviewing. *J Nerv Ment Dis, 155*:410-418, 1972.

Holtzman, W.: Can the computer supplant the clinician? *J Clin Psychol, 16*:119-122, 1960.

Honigfeld, G.: Clinical support functions of computers in psychiatry. *Dis Nerv Syst, 31 (suppl. to #11)*:45-50, 1970.

Impellitteri, J.: Exploration with a computer assisted occupational information system. *Educ Tech, 9*:37-38, 1969.

Katz, M.: Can computers make guidance decisions for students? *College Board Rev, 72*:13-17, 1969.

Knights, R., and Watson, P.: The use of computerized test profiles in neuropsychological assessment. *J Learn Dis, 1*:696-709, 1968.

Klein, D.: Automating the psychiatric case study. *Compr Psychiatry, 11*:518-523, 1970.

Klein, M., Greist, J., and Van Cura, L.: Computers and psychiatry. *Arch Gen Psychiatry, 32*:837-843, 1975.

Kleinmuntz, B.: MMPI decision rules for the identification of college maladjustment. *Psychol Monogr 77 (#14)*:1-22, 1963.

Kleinmuntz, B.: Sign and seer. *J Abnorm Psychol, 72*:163-165, 1967.

Koson, D., Kitchen, C., Kochen, M., and Stodolsky, D.: Psychological testing by computer. *Educ Psychol Meas, 30*:803-810, 1970.

Lang, P.: The on-line computer in behavior therapy research. *Am Psychol, 24*:236-239, 1962.

Lester, D., Kendra, J., Thisted, R., and Perdue, W.: Prediction of homicide with the Rorschach. *J Clin Psych, 31*:752, 1975.

Loehlin, J: *Computer Models of Personality.* New York, Random House, 1968.

Loughary, J., Friesen, D., and Hurst, R.: Autocoun. *Pers Guid J, 45*:6-15, 1966.

Lovaas, O., and Simmons, J.: *Manipulation of Self-destruction in Three Retarded Children.* UCLA, unpublished, 1968.

Marks, P., and Seeman, W.: *The Acturial Description of Abnormal*

Personality. Baltimore, Williams & Wilkins, 1963.
McGuire, M., Lorch, S., and Quarton, G.: Man-machine natural language exchanges based on selected features of unrestricted input. *J Psychiatr Res, 5*:179-191, 1967.
Meehl, P.: Reactions, reflections, projections. In J. Butcher (Ed.) *Objective Personality Assessment.* New York, Academic, 1972. pp. 131-189.
Melhus, G., Hershenson, D., and Vermillion, M.: Computer assisted versus traditional vocational counseling with high and low readiness clients. *J Vocat Behav, 3*:137-144, 1973.
Mendels, R.: The prediction of response to electrolonvulsive therapy. *Amer J Psychiat, 124*:153-159, 1967.
Minor, F., Myers, R., and Super, D.: An experimental computer-based educational and career exploration system. *Pers Guid J, 47*:564-569, 1969.
Paitich, D.: A comprehensive automated psychological examination and report. *Behav Sci, 18*:131-136, 1973.
Pearce, K.: Computer simulation as an aid to the planning of psychiatric services. *Can Psychiatr Assoc J, 2*:219-221, 1967.
Piotrowski, Z.: A digital computer interpretation of inkblot test data. *Psychiatr Q, 38*:1-26, 1964.
Simpson, R.: Goal setting in therapy using computerized feedback. *Diss Abstr Int, 33B*:3360-3361, 1973.
Slack, W.: Computer-based interviewing system dealing with nonverbal behavior as well as keyboard responses. *Science, 171*:84-87, 1971.
Slack, W., and Van Cura, L: Patient reaction to computer-based medical interviewing. *Comput Biomed Res, 1*:527-531, 1968.
Smith, M.: The computer and the TAT. *J School Psychol, 6*:206-214, 1968.
Smith, R.: Examination by computer. *Behav Sci, 8*:76-79, 1965.
Spitzer, R., and Endicott, J.: DIAGNO II. *Am J Psychiatry, 125* [*suppl.*]:12-21, 1969.
Stodolsky, D.: The computer as psychotherapist. *Int J Man-Machine Studies, 2*:327-350, 1970.
Stone, P., Dunphy, D., Smith, M., and Ogilvie, D.: *The General Inquirer.* Unpublished paper, MIT, 1967.
Stroebel, C., and Glueck, B.: Computer derived global judgments in psychiatry. *Am J Psychiatry, 126*:1057-1066, 1970.
Stunden, A.: Computer-simulation of therapy. *J Am Speech Hearing Assoc, 8*:100-104, 1966.
Tiedman, D.: *Can a Machine Develop a Carreer?* Unpublished dissertation, Harvard University, 1969.
Webb, J., Miller, M., and Fowler, R.: Extending professional time. *J Clin Psychol, 26*:210-214, 1970.
Weizenbaum, J.: Eliza. *Community ACM, 9*:36-45, 1966.
Weizenbaum, J.: *Computer Power and Human Reason.* San Francisco, Freeman, 1976.
Youst, D.: The Rochester career guidance project. *Educ Tech, 9*:39-42, 1969.

Chapter 4

PSYCHOTHERAPY BY PRINTED WORD

WRITING as a mode for psychotherapy has many precedents such as Freud's (1954) correspondance with Fliess and his written associations to his own dreams, and Farrow's (1948) suggestion of the use of written free associations in assisting self-analysis. Freud (1959) guided the interpretation of Little Hans' behavior by advising Hans' father by letter, and Rangell (1950) has reported a similar case. Also, many persons regularly write to columnists in newspapers, such as "Ann Landers," for advice.

SOME CASE STUDIES

Grotjahn (1955) reported an exchange of letters with an adolescent girl whose analysis had to be interrupted (but which was eventually resumed). The patient initiated the exchange of letters. Grotjahn categorized his aims in the written communications as to support and encourage the patient and to stay in contact with her. Grotjahn felt that the letters also enabled the patient to continue to work through her problems and to facilitate her return for later analysis. Grotjahn felt that the letters also enabled the patient to continue to work through her problems and to facilitate her return for later analysis. Grotjahn felt that the letters had a limited value and did not play a part in the later analysis, but on the other hand, they did not act as obstacles in the later analysis or affect the formation of her transference neurosis. Grotjahn's patient felt that the distance between her and the psychoanalyst was not changed appreciably by switching to written communication. Grotjahn noted that his interpretations in the letters were general, though not necessarily shallow or banal. He noted also that resistance by the patient could not be handled as well in letters as it can in face-to-face psychotherapy.

Alston (1957) reported a deliberate attempt to use correspondance in order to psychoanalyze a patient who was suffering from tuberculosis and for whom office visits were impossible. (Furthermore, the patient's voice was too weak to allow her to talk.) Letters were exchanged daily for two years. Alston noted several disadvantages. (1) The delay of days between the patient's description of an emotion-laden event and receipt of a reply. (2) The absence of nonverbal cues for the psychoanlyst which led to more misunderstanding than is customary. It is interesting to note in this connection that Ellis (1965) has noted that this particular feature of written psychotherapy is useful for research purposes. The separate effects of the different aspects of psychotherapy can be explored. (3) The patient wrote the letters for eventual publication, since she expected that the psychoanalyst would publish them. This led her to be self-conscious as she wrote. (4) There was an increase in secondary elaboration especially for the purpose of being coherent. Alston noted that these qualities of the correspondance can be utilized by the patient in the service of resistance.

On the positive side Alston noted: (1) Psychotherapy would have been impossible by any other means. (2) The greater distance involved in the correspondance therapy helped to overcome the patient's hostility and fear of psychotherapy. (3) The patient was fixated at a narcissistic level and was able to invest a tremendous amount of libidinal energy in the writing. In face-to-face psychotherapy, she might have been threatened by fantasies of incorporation of the psychotherapist.

Patients often bring written productions to psychotherapy sessions and these are viewed psychodynamically as gifts or as resistances. But writing develops later in childhood and so is free from superego restrictions. Thus, as Alston noted, the patient can often write things which she would resist saying. For Alston's patient, the writing also focussed her upon her survival wishes and assisted her to survive.

Alston noted how his patient wrote for eventual publication and how this affected the quality of her letters. Harrower (1965) has commented upon the ethics of publishing such material with, but especially without, the patient's permission.

DEAF PATIENTS AND DEAF PSYCHOTHERAPISTS

Farber (1953) is a deaf psychotherapist who is therefore forced to use written communications. His patients type or write during the psychotherapy session and Farber responds verbally. Farber who had experience of verbal psychotherapy before he lost his hearing reported that he felt the revised technique had no effect on the success of his psychotherapy. Resistance to the technique quickly vanished within a couple of sessions. Farber noted that nonverbal cues were present and slips of the pen or typewriter were common, and so the interview remained rich in content.

Farber noted several advantages to his technique. (1) The slowing of the tempo of psychotherapy gave Farber more time to digest what was said, and often allowed the patient, for example, to note the repetitiveness of what he was saying. Farber noted that the duration of treatment is not related to how fast one can talk. (2) For people with a visual memory, recollection of what has been said is easier. Also a record exists for confirmation, especially in cases of denial or forgetting. (3) There is a heightened sense of participation. Farber identified with the patients as they typed each word, and he attributed this identification to his paying greater attention to each word rather than listening for key words.

Ellis (1965) has used a similar technique when he has had laryngitis or when he has had deaf patients, and he has written his responses to the patient. Ellis noted that the method was time consuming and that some patients were afraid to commit their thoughts to paper. On the other hand, they could take their messages home to study.

COUNSELING BY MEANS OF AN ADVICE COLUMN

Many daily newspapers carry an advice column, in which readers send in letters to a "counselor." These letters are then printed in the newspaper together with a reply from the "counselor." Many such columns seem to be dominated by humor and the demonstration of sharp wit and plain speech on the part of the counselor, but the advice column can move beyond mere theatrics.

Kesen (1962) has noted that an advice column is greatly different from traditional counseling. The technique obviously lacks the face-to-face or personal relationship that counseling usually involves for the client and the counselor. The interaction is usually restricted to a one-time communication, in which the client receives only one answer. Furthermore, the solution to the client's problem does not come from the client but from the counselor, and therefore it might be expected that the client will achieve less insight and be less likely to follow the advice than if he himself had produced the solution. Kesen noted that the relationship between letter writer and counselor in an advice column is not really a psychotherapeutic relationship, although it may stimulate the client to seek face-to-face counseling.

Although the advice column is limited by considerations of space, the orientation of the counselor can shape the responses. The counselor can be nondirective or directive. He can take a religious or a psychological approach. Kesen himself gave explanations and suggestions to his clients and then led them into a theological orientation. He felt that he was not overly directive or decisive. He tried to be educational rather than sensational.

Kesen noted that some clients felt freer in expressing themselves through writing to his advice column than in face-to-face relationships. In addition, Kesen did not rule out face-to-face encounters. Two of his clients found out where he lived and visited him for personal counseling.

One of Kesen's cases which illustrates his approach concerns a church member who went to visit a friend who had lost her daughter in a traffic accident. She was refused admission to the friend's house. This deeply disappointed her, because she had hoped to share the consolation she had received from Christianity when she had been in a similar situation.

Kesen, in his reply to her, noted that people do not always respond as we would like. He described the general psychological characteristics of the bereaved person, such as feeling guilt and hostility toward others. He suggested visiting the person to show sympathy, rather than forcing the Christian faith upon the bereaved person. Only after sufficient rapport has been established might it be possible to communicate one's belief in Christianity.

SPONTANEOUS WRITING BY CLIENTS

Kew and Kew (1963) have noted that clients can be encouraged to abandon conscious control and to write spontaneously whatever comes into their mind, much as in the process of free association used by psychoanalysts. The thoughts can be jotted down whenever they occur and enlarged upon later in the day, perhaps at a regular time set aside for this purpose.

The writings should not be analyzed by the client, but rather he should forget them until his session with the counselor. To ponder over them too much may merely confuse the patient. In the counseling session, it is often useful to have the client free associate to what he has written. However, the patient should feel free to delay showing them to the counselor and to postpone discussing them, if he so chooses.

Resistance is often manifest. For example, clients may forget to bring their notes with them to the counseling session. Often the client feels anxious about the counselor's reaction to the notes, and he may call, perhaps to confirm the next appointment but also to feel out whether the counselor has read the notes and what he thinks about them. For some clients, it is easier to write in the third person. Sometimes, extensive note writing itself can be a form of resistance.

Some clients experience too much anxiety with this technique. The anxiety may lay in the repressed material or when the associations to the material are painful. Note writing is obviously counter-productive for such clients. Kew and Kew emphasized that note writing should be used only to facilitate psychotherapy and not to replace spontaneous verbalization.

Kew and Kew reported the case of a twenty-two-year-old female who was depressed and drank heavily. Her counselor asked her to write down her thoughts whenever she had the urge to drink. She refused at first, but then did so. Then she refused to let the counselor read the notes; eventually she permitted him to read them silently; then aloud; and finally to discuss them with her. The note-writing cut down on her drinking and led to some self-insight, thereby facilitating psychotherapy. The note writing was a form of cartharsis; it helped her test the counselor and increased her confidence in him; it facilitated the development of positive transference; and it permitted her to express herself with less fear and guilt.

Kew and Kew noted that note writing often helps to break the ice for clients who don't know where to begin or what to say. It is useful for clients who have too much fear and embarrassment to express some thoughts out loud. It is easier for some clients to think of associations and fantasies alone than when with the counselor, thereby speeding up the process of psychotherapy. The client may be able to accept his problem sooner for he may find that recalling past experiences is not as devastating as he imagined. Thus, he may become more able to handle this material with the counselor. Note writing helps release pent-up emotions, especially toward the counselor (both positive and negative emotions). The note writing also helps guide the counselor, both from the content of the material and from an awareness of how the patient feels about his psychotherapy. It also enables both the counselor and the client to observe the progress being made.

Ellis (1965) has also encouraged clients to make notes on their problems and the process of their psychotherapy and to bring these notes to the counseling sessions for use there. Burton (1965) has suggested that ordinary prose writing might enable clients to grow, much as authors themselves grow through writing. The sharing of the creative work by the counselor and the client may also deepen the psychotherapeutic encounter.

The use of writing has been formalized in some systems of psychotherapy. For example, in fixed-role therapy (Kelly, 1955), the client is asked to write out a self-description. This self-description is used to help identify the client's major constructs and write a fixed role for him to play during the next stage of the psychotherapy. Mair (1970) has discussed in a very general way the possibility of having two people write sketches of each other and then discuss the sketches in a personal encounter. However, he does not appear to have utilized this technique in psychotherapy yet; he presented the notion more as a model for psychological investigation.

BIBLIOTHERAPY

McKinney (1975) noted that reading can be recreational and relaxing; it can furnish glimpses of self-understanding; it can lead to changes in our attitudes; and it may be a stimulus for identification with the fictional characters thereby offering suggestions for solving our own problems. Fiction can also make us aware of, and partially satisfy, our unconscious (as well as conscious) needs.

If the reader can identify with the character in the work of fiction and experience an emotional release, the experience may be cathartic (Menninger, 1937). For these experiences to have a lasting effect, the client may need to discuss and work through these feelings with a psychotherapist. McKinney noted, however, that research on the effects of watching aggressive films does not indicate the existence of a cathartic effect (Aronson, 1972).

McKinney uses fiction to supplement conventional psychotherapy. He uses short stories which can be read in a single sitting and so do not disturb the client's schedule or sleeping pattern. He also permits the client a choice, trusting that the client may select the story most appropriate for his own needs. It is not always easy for the psychotherapist to find the right book for each client.

Gottschalk (1948) noted that bibliotherapy would also help the client to understand psychological terminology, therefore facilitating communication with the psychotherapist. Bibliotherapy may help stimulate the client to verbalize problems which are associated with shame and guilt, since he may see that others have similar problems. Bibliotherapy may help the client think constructively between sessions, and it may reinforce social values and behavior by presenting examples.

Gottschalk noted that bibliotherapy worked best if the client had sought psychotherapy (rather than being forced into psychotherapy), if he was in the habit of reading and had good intellectual ability, and if the disorder was mild (a psychoneurosis or personality disorder). (Incidentally, it is clear that McKinney is talking about the reading of fiction, whereas Gottschalk is talking about the reading of psychological texts.*)

In recent years a number of psychotherapists have explored the use of poems in psychotherapy as an agent of communication between psychotherapist and patient (Chase, 1973; Leedy, 1969, 1973). For some patients, it is easier to communicate important messages either through their own poetry or through the use of the poems of others. Poems may be used to inspire, confront, stimulate, and unblock. Chase noted, however, that when the group leader is unskilled, the use of poetry can increase the patients' arrogance and the self/ideal-self discrepancy.

Some psychotherapists recommend for their patients the use of "literary gems" (Likorish, 1975), brief quotations relevant to their problems which they can carry with them and refer to during the day.

Likorish (1975) has pointed to the benefits of reading for the psychotherapist himself. Reading fiction can facilitate the cultivation of empathy in the psychotherapist (Mahoney, 1965). Fiction evokes feelings, and the psychotherapist may come to a greater understanding of himself and others if he stays alert to these feelings. Fiction provides the psychotherapist with vicarious experiences of characters and situations that he may not himself encounter in his life. Fiction may guide the psychotherapist in a search for values. It may sharpen his psychological wits (Royce, 1970) and enable him to probe more deeply into human motivation. The symbolism in fiction may also help him better understand the symbolic world of his clients.

---

*Rational-emotive therapists often assign psychological materials with illustrative cases to their clients on the theory of rational emotive therapy (Ellis, 1965).

THE WRITTEN SUMMARY IN GROUP PSYCHOTHERAPY

Yalom et al. (1975) noted that group psychotherapy sessions often end on a emotional note and leave the participants bewildered about what has taken place. Integration of the events of the session is often difficult. In order to deal with this issue, Yalom began preparing a detailed summary of each group meeting that was mailed to each group member prior to the next meeting. The group leader who prepares the summary may add editorial comment, and the summaries average three to seven double-spaced typewritten pages.

What are the advantages of such a technique? Yalom noted that many patients feel a great deal of anxiety in group psychotherapy sessions. This anxiety can be contained by providing some structure, such as providing a written agenda for each meeting, didactic teaching during the group meeting, and video playbacks. The written summary was found to be the most effective approach to reducing anxiety in the group members.

The summaries provide a number of other functions.

(1) They provide the patients with some understanding of what happens in the group.
(2) They reward the patients for improvements in their behavior.
(3) They tend to prevent maladaptive behavior such as absenteeism.
(4) They encourage silent members of the group to participate and the slower members to move.
(5) They promote group cohesiveness by noting the similarities between the different group members and by pointing to the caring of each member for the others.
(6) They are didactic and provide an opportunity to make interpretations, both to emphasize interpretations already made and to make new interpretations.
(7) They provide a new perspective on the group psychotherapy meeting.
(8) They increase the hope of the group members by point-

ing out that the group is not chaotic and incoherent, but that it does indeed have coherence and purpose.

Yalom noted that the summary serves to revivify the group. Group members often forget the group meetings during their week and anything that serves to remind them of the group and the events that take place during the group meetings should facilitate therapeutic movement.

It is important that the members of a psychotherapy group reflect upon the experience of the group meeting. One of the tasks of the group leader is to provide some reflection upon the events of the group and to structure them for greater understanding by the group members. The written summary serves to rekindle the experiences that took place in the previous group meeting and to permit the individual group members to reflect upon them, often with less intense emotions than they experienced during the original experience. Thus, the group members may be able to reinterpret and restructure the group experience themselves at this later point in time.

The group leader can use the summary to repeat interpretations that might have been missed by the group members during the heat of the group meeting. The group leader can also use the summary to make interpretations that he missed making during the original meeting. The summary also encourages the group members to comment upon the summary and the original experience at the beginning of the next group meeting.

Yalom has pointed out that one important factor in group psychotherapy is the establishment of group norms that facilitate therapeutic movement. The group leader shapes these norms, explicitly and implicitly. He may reinforce some behaviors and ignore others. He may teach, set ground rules, and act as a model for the other group members. He can also use the written summary to augment these procedures.

By judicious selection of what the group leader reports in the summary, he can provide himself with "therapeutic leverage." If a patient, for example, makes a key revelation or achieves some self-insight, the group leader can take care to repeat this in the summary. The group leader can make interpretations that he was unable to make at the time or that he was unaware of at the time. Because the group leader maintains a longer range perspective on the therapy process, he can point to cyclical patterns in the behavior of the group or of some group member. He can point to changes in the members' behaviors that have occurred.

The written summary also provides a means for the psychotherapist to make self-disclosures that hopefully serve the group's needs rather than his own. Perhaps his self-disclosures facilitate model setting, deepen the relationship between him and the group members, demonstrate a belief in the usefulness of therapy, and facilitate transference.

The written summary also fills in gaps for group members and co-therapists who miss meetings. It also helps new members enter an on-going group.

The written summary is an event in the group, and the group members respond to this event in their characteristic styles. This behavior can then be discussed in the group, much as the reactions to other events are discussed.

Yalom noted that the written summaries helped the group leaders. The knowledge that they have a "second chance" helped them relax during the group meetings and lessened their tendency to control the group. That the group leader also has to review each group meeting forces him to make his interpretations carefully and clearly. The summaries also facilitate supervision.

Over 90 percent of the group members surveyed found the summaries useful and wanted them to continue. Yalom and his colleagues noted that the summaries served also to demystify the psychotherapy experience and facilitated the establishment of an egalitarian relationship between psychotherapist and patient. Yalom and Elkins (1974) have described an extension of this idea to face-to-face individual therapy. The psychotherapist and the patient both made summaries after each session of psychotherapy. The patient and psychotherapist exchanged these summaries from time to time, and they explored the impact of these events upon the process of psychotherapy.

RESEARCH OF THE EFFECTIVENESS OF PSYCHOTHERAPY BY PRINTED WORD

Bastien and Jacobs (1973) took a sample of volunteer college students and conducted psychotherapy by mail with each of them for a period of four month. One group received behaviorally oriented therapeutic responses from the counselor, another group received reassurance responses, and a control group was asked merely to regularly check their problems on a problem check list and mail the list to the counselor. The group receiving the behaviorally oriented therapeutic responses showed a significant decrease in problems over the four months, whereas those receiving reassurance and those in the control group did not.

Widroe and Davidson (1961) took twelve female psychiatric in-patients diagnosed as schizophrenics or neurotics and had them keep daily schedules of their activities which they were to bring to their psychotherapist each day. The psychotherapist always asked for the schedule, sometimes commented upon it, and sometimes read it aloud. Widroe and Davidson noted several attitudes toward the writing in the patients. (1) Some invested the schedule with the magical presence of the psychotherapist. (2) Others invested the schedule with directive powers similar to those of a demanding superego. (3) For some, the schedule became a focus around which the patients were able to direct feeling at the psychotherapist which they were not able to express verbally. For example, one patient, who was angry at the psychotherapist, tore up her schedule. (4) For some, the schedule modified ego functions by strengthening some defenses and emphasizing secondary process thinking. The writing imposed direction and form that tended to suppress ideation that was not part of the pattern and to build up compulsive defenses. (5) Since the written schedules were durable, they could be reread, and, often on rereading, the patients' affect was modified: for example, anxiety often declined. (6) The writing of schedules also encouraged interpersonal activity, for the persons in the project began to function as a group with writing as the group activity.

Burton (1965) noted that schizophrenics often find face-to-face psychotherapy threatening, and the use of written communications may facilitate the therapeutic encounter. For these patients, to reject the writing, freely given, is to reject the patient.

The project instituted by Widroe and Davidson has some similarities to the Morita therapy popular in Japan. As part of Morita therapy, the patient keeps a methodical diary which is collected daily and in which the psychotherapist writes comments and reactions (Kora and Ohara, 1973).

DISCUSSION

Burnell and Motelet (1973) distinguished three sets of conditions that lead to the use of written communications between psychotherapist and patient.

(1) The first set of conditions are those based on physical circumstances. When the patient or psychotherapist must be away for a prolonged absence, when patient or psychotherapist transfers to a new area and the patient needs support to follow through with a new psychotherapist, when the patient lives in an isolated area and visits are infrequent, when psychotherapy is indirect, using the help of a relative or friend who has access to a distant patient, or when the patient is considered dangerous to himself or others and knowledge about his whereabouts is considered useful.

(2) The next set of conditions are based on transference or countertransference. When the patient wishes to avoid expressing negative or positive feelings toward the psychotherapist in the course of psychotherapy, when the patient wishes to gain the psychotherapist's approval by producing creative writings to express deeply felt experiences, when the patient has difficulty facing the termination of psychotherapy and chooses the written word to avoid an intense affective experience, when the patient wishes to give a follow-up report after termination (which may also help reduce the separation anxiety),

when the psychotherapist wishes to clarify the current status of a patient who cancels or does not show for psychotherapy or carry out treatment recommendations, or when the patient's obsessiveness compels him to structure or resist the psychotherapy sessions by bringing in written material.
(3) The last conditions are based on communication problems: When the patient has a special talent, inclination, or ability to express himself in writing; when the patient is deaf or unable to speak; or when the therapist is deaf or unable to speak.

Psychotherapy using the printed word has many unique features (but it must be remembered that not all of the features discussed below apply to every use of the printed word described above). The use of writing for psychotherapeutic interaction slows the tempo of psychotherapy. It delays feedback both from patient to psychotherapist and vice versa. This allows for greater reflection on the material communicated and encourages thinking and analysis. It has even been suggested that this encouragement of reflection on the part of the patient may make his interaction with the psychotherapist of less importance to him and so may promote self-treatment.

A second major quality of writing in psychotherapy is that there is a greater focus on cognitive and intellectual processes for, though affect is not eliminated, it is reduced. Writing encourages secondary process thinking. Related to this, the use of letter writing in psychotherapy makes it more difficult for the psychotherapist to assess the affective intensity of the patient's communications.

Although the use of letter writing for psychotherapy eliminates many nonverbal cues that the face-to-face psychotherapist can attend to, nonverbal behaviors do exist. The mailing and writing behavior (such as spelling) can give cues to the patient's mental status, resistance, distancing, or dependence on the psychotherapist. As has been noted above, the use of letter writing does not eliminate such psychodynamic processes as transference, countertransference, and resistance.

The use of writing encourages thinking and introspection

rather than action. Thus, as has been noted above, some structured writing tasks for patients can be used to build up compulsive defenses. Writing reduces spontaneity, and the patient will tend to be more cautious and to elaborate his thoughts more. It may promote impulse control. For certain kinds of patients, this emphasis may be beneficial.

The psychotherapist who does psychotherapy by letter may become anxious from his reduced ability to monitor and increase impulse control in his patient and from the possibility of losing contact with the patient. However, in preparing his response, the psychotherapist has more time for consultation and review which may reduce his anxiety. The tendency to be cautious and to elaborate in letters may make the psychotherapist's interpretation more general and so less effective.

Because the psychotherapist is not met face-to-face in psychotherapy by letter, the patient can build fantasies about the psychotherapist. This may be helpful if the patient can fantasize a psychotherapist of the kind that he needs for resolution of his problems, a kind that the actual psychotherapist may not match in reality. On the other hand, the patient's fantasies may be such as to impede treatment.

Some psychotherapists see writing as a defense from the honesty of direct confrontation and as a resistance. But if writing is creative it can work counter to defenses. It may also be cathartic. Letter writing is a solitary activity (which leads some psychotherapists to view it as a dissociative activity). However, there are probably some people who find it easier to communicate by letter, either as a general habit or at times in order to communicate particular thoughts. Clearly, some patients may be unable to use writing effectively for psychotherapy and some psychotherapists may be unable to respond appropriately.

Since the writing can be kept, it allows for a record of the psychotherapy. It permits review and rehearsal. Some psychotherapists maintain that the use of diaries and notes can shorten the period needed for psychotherapy. Furthermore, the writings of the patient can provide material for analysis, as do dreams. On the other hand, the immutability of the written word does make the medium too anxiety provoking for some patients.

Clearly, no one would advocate the various aspects of psychotherapy using writing that have been described in this book for all patients. But for some patients with some problems with some psychotherapists, the use of writing in its various manifestations provides a powerful tool in the psychotherapist's armamentarium.

APPENDIX 1: WRITING ANONYMOUS LETTERS

This chapter has reviewed the use of written communications in psychotherapy in which a writer and respondent interact. It has been argued that such communications can be helpful to the client. Clients can also be helped on occasions even if the counselor never responds to the client. The mere ventilation of the client's problems in a letter which is sent to the counselor can help alleviate the client's distress.

The following is one of a series of letters sent to a psychologist who was teaching a psychology course on television. The letters were sent anonymously, and there was no way that the instructor of the course could respond to the client. (The televized lectures had been prerecorded, many months prior to their broadcast.) The letter reproduced below is a typical letter from the series.

Sunday Morning
Hello Professor. Hey it looks like I'm going to make it through the weekend. You've got to say this for me — I fight like hell.

It seems incredible that I should be doing something quite so insane as this. I thought I had better sense and control.

Incidentally I was diagnosed by Doctor . . . . a number of years ago after a complête psychological evaluation as psychoneurotic, hysteric. They're even nasty sounding words. God, how I hate myself. What are you thinking at this point — boy what a lulu! If you're reading these at all, which I suspect if you're getting them you are with avid interest stemming from intellectual curiosity. Do you perhaps feel sorry for my family right now? If you feel sorry for me forget it. Remember pity is unprofessional. With all the shrinks I ever met, there was only one who didn't break down and show pity at one time or another. When they did, that turned me off immediately. I'd find I couldn't tell them anything that was difficult from then on. Of course, the one who didn't was the last one and that one eventually got somewhere — not, obviously not, all the way, but farther than he thought. He wasn't really a shrink though, he was a psychologist. He was tremendous, but I still hate him for pushing me out and for being wrong about hypnosis. Yet, I'd give my eyeteeth to go back into therapy with him now with the knowledge and awareness of my feelings and returning of memory. But that clinic is closed. So it seems are all the others, with one exception, around here.

I'm not exactly proud of this, but at this point I don't care that much either, but I've spent most of the weekend fantasizing that you made the effort, found me and came up with some way of getting me help. But, I guess that doesn't really surprise you, does it. Oh to have somebody out there care, somebody see something in me worth redeeming, somebody think I were important enough to help. But the reality of the situation is that I am one among droves of people needing help and there just isn't enough money, time, or caring to go around. The reality doesn't help, though. It doesn't make the pain go away. Nor does it help with self-loathing. Nor does it help dissolve the walls. That's what I hate the most — the walls between men and health, people, etc. To be so crippled by the trauma that I must always be prepared to defend. It seems that somehow I should be able to overcome.

My husband is not overly happy about the thought of my going back into therapy. He knows it led before to my leaving my first husband and he's afraid he'll lose me. On the other hand he becomes upset because I can't be happy and disassociate him with other men. He also seems to have some feelings that his love should be enough. But if he had the kind of love for me that would fill the need, we couldn't truly be man and wife. Somehow, there must be a way to learn to live without a father's love. My husband is too important to me as lover, companion, provider, etc. to jeopardize that. He is the one person in the world I could tell how I felt — but I'm not these days. It would only upset him too much. And he tries so hard to make me happy. But I'm not allowed to be happy. And, I don't know why.

This is not exactly a model of English Comp., is it? Buts and Ands all over the place.

Is there any help for someone like me? If the therapy were available have you the knowledge now? You know no one did 20 years ago. Does anyone now? I wish I could get your answer to those questions. I wish I could even know that you are getting these.

Incidentally, in case you haven't guessed, I'm just writing down the thoughts as they come. I'm not even re-reading this. If you're going to read anything, you might as well get the unvarnished truth.

My husband just called. It's time to go pick him up from church.

Funny how much better writing all this makes me feel.

                            Your friendly neighborhood crackpot
Hope and Fear

APPENDIX 2: MORITA THERAPY

Morita therapy is one of the few systems of psychotherapy that incorporates writing into the psychotherapeutic process, and it is therefore of interest to explore the use of writing in Morita therapy in some depth. This description is based upon Kora (1965).

Morita therapy was developed by Shoma Morita (1853-1923) and first described in print in 1917. It was first practiced in Japan. Morita therapy is designed for the treatment of some forms of neurosis, primarily neurasthenia, phobias, and anxiety neurosis. The following are goals of treatment.

(1) to make the patient understand the nature of his symptoms;
(2) to help the patient achieve the state of "arugamama," which closely resembles the state of Zen indifference. To achieve this state, the patient must admit the nature of his symptoms and the anxiety associated with them; he must accept his symptoms; the patient must behave constructively despite his symptoms; and he must realize that his symptoms are not foreign bodies in him, but that he must suffer the agony by accepting the symptoms.

(3) to stop the patient from trying to be perfect; and
(4) to engage the patient in occupational therapy, which satisfies his need for activity and serves to make him less egocentric.

Treatment is divided into four stages. In the first stage, which lasts about seven days, the patient is confined to bed. He is permitted to leave his bed only for meals and for washing and elimination. He is not permitted visitors, radio, television, smoking, writing, talking, or working. He is encouraged to think, especially about his symptoms, to worry, and to suffer. As this experience becomes excruciating (the patient is bored and restless and suffering from sensory deprivation), the patient moves to stage two. In stage two, the patient is allowed to get up. He is encouraged to observe the world, to engage in light work, and to keep a diary in which to record his observations. This stage lasts about seven days. In the third stage, the patient is encouraged to engage in heavy work around the hospital, work involving manual labor such as carpentry and gardening. He is encouraged to read books on geography, history, and biography. This stage lasts about seven days. In the final stage, which lasts about fourteen days, the patient is prepared for re-entry into his life. He may leave the hospital from time to time, and he engages in complicated work of the kind he does in actual life.

Morita therapy can be compared to various Western psychotherapies and analogies can be drawn between various facets of the therapy and techniques in Western psychotherapies. The reasons for the success of Morita therapy can also be explored using the theoretical rationales of Western psychotherapies. However, here my interest is in the use of the diary in Morita therapy. The following extracts come from a case reported by Kora (1965).

> August 8: The first day out of bed. I could not fall asleep easily last night and tossed back and forth. It may have been past midnight when I fell asleep. Although I didn't have enough sleep, I was awakened in the morning by the loud singing of a drunken man who was walking down the street just outside the hospital. After I woke up, I realized that the

duration from the time I fell asleep to the time I woke up seemed to me like a fleeting moment. I also realized that I did have the feeling of having slept well. This is the first time that I had such a feeling. Although it might be just temporary, I nevertheless am happy about it. [Annotation: A person is bound to get the amount of sleep that is required for him physiologically whether he likes it or not, and so you should leave it to nature whether you get that sleep or not. If you keep up this attitude, you will come to accept sleep naturally without being worried about sleeplessness or without being happy for having slept well.] When I heard somebody say yesterday that he ran out of work, I was worried if there was any work left for me. But when I got up this morning and looked at the dwarfed trees, I saw weeds and withered leaves. [Annotation: If you look at something carefully, you will experience some feeling. Act and work in accordance with that feeling. There is no end in work. You experience inexplicable joy when you examine the work you have done.] When I left the hospital building and went into the yard, I met people as if I were seeing them for the first time. They stunned me, and I blushed. But on second thought, I realized that they were all in the same boat, so to speak. When I realized that, I felt relieved and did not become as stiff as I thought I would. [Annotation: Meet the people just as you are, just as you blush!] While I remained outside, I was haunted by a fear as if I were being chased by something and I felt I was likely to lose my composure. [Annotation: As of the moment, it cannot be helped if your mind should be lacking composure. It is all right even if you were nervous and timid.]
(From Kora, 1965, pp. 631-632)

It can be readily seen that the annotations written in the diary by the therapist resemble closely those that might be made by a Gestalt therapist. The therapist encourages the patient to accept his feelings and his thoughts. The therapist says that it is fine to feel anxiety, boredom, bashfulness, and one should not fight it. The patient is encouraged to go with his feelings rather than against them. (If this is how one feels, then he *should* feel this way.)

It is also readily apparent that the annotations of the therapist aim for the patient to attain Zen indifference. Zen indiffence is not a state of apathy or disinterest. It is a state in which one observes, experiences, and feels, but it is also a state in which one does not act as if driven by his thoughts and his feelings. If one feels anxious, then so be it. He feels, and therefore is, anxious. He accepts it. It is possible to be in a state of Zen indifference and yet be intimately involved in and interested in the world. One is not, however, pushed and pulled by environmental pressures or his own desires.

REFERENCES

Alston, E.: Psychoanalytic psychotherapy conducted by correspondance. *Int J Psychoanal, 38*:32-50, 1957.
Aronson, E.: *The Social Animal.* San Francisco, Freeman, 1972.
Bastein, S. and Jacobs, A.: Dear Sheila. *J Consult Clin Psychol, 42*:151, 1974.
Burnell, G. and Motelet, K.: Correspondance therapy. *Arch Gen Psychiatry, 28*:728-731, 1973.
Burton, A.: The use of written productions in psychotherapy. In L. Pearson (Ed.) *The Use of Written Communications in Psychotherapy.* Springfield, Thomas, 1965.
Chase, J.: Poems struggling to be free. *Human Behav, 2(8)*:24-28, 2973.
Ellis, A.: Some uses of the printed, written, and recorded word in psychotherapy. In L. Pearson (Ed.) *The Use of Written Communication in Psychotherapy.* Springfield, Thomas, 1965.
Farber, J.: Written communication in psychotherapy. *Psychiatry, 16*:365-374, 1953.
Farrow, E.: *Psychoanalyze Yourself.* New York, Intl Univs Pr, 1948.
Freud, S.: *The Origins of Psychoanalysis.* Edited by M. Bonaparte, A. Freud, and E. Kris. New York, Basic, 1954.
Freud, S.: Analysis of a phobia in a five-year-old boy. *Collected Papers,* Volume 3, 149-289. New York, Basic, 1959.
Gottschalk, L.: Bibliotherapy as an adjuvant in psychotherapy. *Am J Psychiatry, 104*:632-637, 1948.
Grotjahn, M.: *Six Letters to an Analyst by an Adolescent Girl.* Unpublished manuscript, 1955.
Harrower, M: Therapeutic communications by letter, notebook and record transcriptions. In L. Pearson (Ed.) *The Use of Written Communications in Psychotherapy.* Springfield, Thomas, 1965. pp. 37-46.
Kelly, G.: *The Psychology of Personal Constructs.* New York, Norton, 1955.
Kesen, S.: The advice column as a means of counseling. *Japan Christian Quart, 28(3)*:168-171, 1962.
Kew, C. and Kew, C.: Writing as an aid in pastoral counseling and psychotherapy. *Pastoral Psychol, 14(Dec.)*:37-43, 1963.

Kora, T.: Morita therapy. *Int J Psychiatry,* 1:611-645, 1965.
Kora T. and Ohara, K.: Morita therapy. *Psychol Today,* 6(10):63-68, 1973.
Leedy, J.: *Poetry Therapy.* Philadelphia, Lippincott, 1969.
Leedy, J.: *Poetry the Healer.* Philadelphia, Lippincott, 1973.
Likorish, J.: The therapeutic use of literature. *Psychother,* 12:105-109, 1975.
Mahoney, S.: The evocative value of fiction for psychotherapists in training. *Psychother,* 2:139-140, 1965.
Mair, J.: Psychologists are human too. In D. Bannister (Ed.): *Perspectives in Personal Construct Theory.* New York, Academic, 1970. pp. 157-184.
McKinney, F.: Explorations in bibliotherapy. *Psychother,* 12:110-117, 1975.
Menninger, W.: Bibliotherapy. *Bull Menninger Clin,* 1:263-274, 1937.
Rangell, L.: A treatment of nightmares in a seven-year-old boy. *Psychoanal Study Child,* 5:358-390, 1950.
Royce, J.: *Toward Unification in Psychology.* Toronto, U of Toronto Pr, 1970.
Widroe, H. and Davidson, J.: The use of directed writing in psychotherapy. *Bull Menninger Clin,* 25:110-119, 1961.
Yalom, I., Brown, S., and Bloch, S.: The written summary as a group psychotherapy technique. *Arch Gen Psychiatry,* 32:605-613, 1975.
Yalom, I. and Elkins, G.: *Every Day Gets a Little Closer.* New York, Basic, 1974.

Chapter 5

THE TAPE RECORDER AND COUNSELING

THE tape recorder has been found to be a useful adjunct in counseling in a number of ways, for example, in psychological testing and in behavior modification. However, the tape recorder has also been used in such a way as to minimize the counselor-client relationship. In fact, using the tape recorder, it has been possible to eliminate the counselor to an even greater extent than by using a computer program to provide feedback to the client. Using the tape recorder, *all* feedback can be eliminated.

First, however, the more technical uses of the tape recorder in counseling should be reviewed.

TAPE RECORDERS AND PSYCHOLOGICAL TESTING

The tape recorder has been used to record test items for psychological testing. Urmer et al. (1960) tape recorded MMPI items and compared the administration of the items by tape recorder and by booklet. They found no differences on any of the clinical scales. The use of the tape recording was felt to fatigue subjects less, to standardize the response speed, and to reduce the confounding effect of written comprehension (that is, poor readers find the test easier). Henning et al. (1972) have reported a similar study of reliability and validity of the MMPI as administered by a tape recorder.

The Brook Reaction Test (Heim and Watts, 1966) is a test that presents words to subjects and requires subjects to make associations to the words. The words are chosen to tap competing interests, such as "bar," which may lead to associations of alcohol, gymnastics, the law, swimming, and so forth. The subject's responses are used to assess his interests. In order to minimize experimenter bias in the administration of the test, Heim and Watts routinely use a tape recorded presentation of the stimulus words.

The tape recorder can also be used to present vocational guidance information in an automated vocational guidance system (see Chapter 4).

TAPE RECORDERS AND BEHAVIOR MODIFICATION

Migler and Wolpe (1967) reported the use of a tape recorder in the systematic desensitization of fear of public speaking. The relaxation instructions and the hierarchy of stimuli were recorded in the patient's own voice. The patient was permitted to take the tape recorder home and to utilize the recordings. His fear of public speaking was greatly reduced.

Denholtz (1970) has described how the tape recorder can be employed in a variety of techniques. For example, in relaxation training, Denholtz has recorded his own relaxation instructions and then given the patient the tape to take home, with instructions to practice with it twice daily. This is particularly useful for patients who are too anxious to "let go" in the presence of the therapist. Some patients learn to relax at home first and then are able to relax later when in the therapist's office.

With systematic desensitization, Denholtz adds scenes from the hierarchy immediately after the relaxation instructions. Usually he tapes one scene from the hierarchy at a time, but occasionally he may tape more. The patient is instructed to use the tape recording daily until the next session, at which time he usually reports no anxiety to the taped scenes. Denholtz reports that he cuts the number of visits for each step in the hierarchy from an average of over five to an average of two by using the tape recorder. To prevent anxiety being conditioned to the taped scene, Denholtz tells his patients to use the tape recorder only once or twice a day and never when they are aware of significant amounts of anxiety.

In covert sensitization, the patient is asked to imagine some disgusting scene which induces nausea, while also imagining some undesirable behavior that he wishes to eliminate (Cautela,

1966). Again, the induction of nausea through imagery and the pairing of this nausea with imagination of the undesirable behavior can be tape recorded and the tape recording used at home. Denholtz noted that such practice reduced blocking and the wandering of thoughts during the treatment.

Finally, Denholtz uses tape recordings in flooding (Stampfl and Levis, 1968). Denholtz noted that the creation of the anxiety-evoking situation was quite draining for him, and the use of a tape recorded presentation eliminates this strain. He tape records his initial presentation of the scene and then plays the tape repeatedly in his office. Because flooding has a distressing effect on the patient, patients are never given these tapes to use at home until there has been considerable abatement of the initially intense anxiety.*

To illustrate the use of the tape recorder, Denholtz presented the case of a twenty-six-year-old woman who was depressed and doubted that she loved her recently-wedded husband. She had constant thoughts about her ex-lover with whom she had broken up some two years previously. Denholtz asked the patient to imagine herself with her ex-lover and about to have sexual intercourse. She was to imagine her lover suddenly going next door and jumping into a cesspool full of urine and feces, then, trying to pull her into the cesspool and splashing feces and urine over her. The scene evoked considerable disgust in the patient. The session was taped and the patient advised to use the tape twice daily. A week later, a different scene was evoked — her ex-lover as the epitome of all the things she disliked in men. Again, she was asked to use the tape recording twice daily. After another week she reported that she was no longer troubled by thoughts of her ex-lover. Not all of the patient's problems were resolved, of course, but the removal of the obsession freed her to return to work and to function domestically and sexually with her husband. The total office time spent with the patient was one hour.

Denholtz and Mann (1975) have described a completely automated behavior therapy program that can be administered by

---

*Films and tape recordings can also be used for modeling in behavior therapy.

nonprofessionals. They reported treating flight phobias, using a muscle relaxation training tape and a film that presented a hierarchy of anxiety-provoking scenes, with each followed by a pleasurable scene. There were also instruction tapes. Of those who completed the program, about 80 percent were able to fly.

Donner and Guerney (1969) compared systematic desensitization of test-taking anxiety carried out in a group format by a counselor and by a set of tape recorded instructions. Both treatment groups experienced a reduction in test-taking anxiety as compared to a no-treatment group. There was, however, a tendency for the treatment group with the therapist present to achieve higher grades on subsequent tests than the treatment group with the therapist absent, when both groups were given the same number of sessions. With more sessions, however, the tape recorded treatment method might prove equally effective.

TALKING TO A TAPE RECORDER AS THERAPY

Maslow (1970) reported seeing a college student for one hour of counseling in which he never said one word. The woman talked without his responding, and at the end of the hour thanked him for his help and left. He noted that he, a therapist, was present in the room and he was obviously interested in what she said. Thus, he indicated by this minimal behavior that he felt that the client was worthy. The client felt safe, protected, less vulnerable, and less anxious. The therapist had not scolded her. He was seen by the client as someone on her side. Perhaps there was an unconscious realization in the client of being liked, protected, and respected.

Slack (1960) reported a similar experience. He paid delinquent boys to talk into a tape recorder. The boys were paid one dollar an hour to talk about their dreams and fantasies. An interviewer was present but was initially unobtrusive. Slack noted that the boys became less hostile in time, became attached to him (positive transference), attended more regularly, and showed less involvement with delinquent behavior.

Schwitzgebel (1964) tried a similar experiment, except that his boys were permitted to talk about anything they wished.

Again, however, the interviewer began by being unobtrusive and again the boys became attached to the interviewer. They attended regularly and became less involved in delinquent behavior. In Schwitzgebel's experiment, however, there were other aspects to the program: gifts of food and cigaretts, group discussions, card games, and group tasks such as rewriting the driver's handbook for the driving test to help the boys pass the driving test. Thus, we cannot be sure that the talking into the tape recorder was the primary cause of the behavior change. Schwitzgebel noted that the boys were given an honest job (being subjects in a research study). The job was not busy-work and it was not described as therapy. In a follow-up study (Schwitzgebel, 1963), it was found that a similar proportion of delinquent boys in the project had been arrested as delinquent boys not in the project. However, those boys in the project who had been arrested, had been arrested less often and spent less time in detention than the delinquent boys not in the project.

In an extension of this idea, Stollak and Guerney (1964) had delinquents talk for half and hour at a time into a tape recorder, with no counselor present. They were told to talk about their feelings and thoughts and to help the counselor understand their delinquency. The counselor later listened to the tape recordings but never commented on them to the delinquents.

Stollak and Guerney noted that positive transference occurred. The delinquents showed curiosity about the counselor and were attracted to him. They would ask him when they would be seeing him next. The delinquents were regular in attendance (they were in detention at the time), eager, cooperative, and impressively introspective at times. The delinquents initially expressed a good deal of hostility toward the center. Perhaps as a result of the fact that they were not punished for the expression of their hostility, they began to open up and to reveal more about their feelings. The delinquents probably felt that they were receiving support and acceptance.

Of twelve delinquents who were recruited, two refused to participate and one was afraid to be left alone and wanted the counselor present. One other delinquent was extremely negativistic. For the remaining delinquents, the involvement with the counselor was a source of pride, and it was socially acceptable. Much of the following resistance was evident in the "therapy" sessions: saying nothing; shutting off the recorder and playing with it; bringing comics and playing cards into the room; going to the bathroom; and opening the door to peer out. Clearly, the procedure aroused anxiety.

Stollak and Guerney noted therapeutic movement in the delinquents. They moved from talking about hostility to talking of their feelings of depression and worthlessness. The "therapy" seemed more useful for those of higher intelligence (though the highest intelligence was 105, with a mean for the delinquents of 91). The positive effect of the "therapy" decreased over the sessions (a maximum of seventeen were held).

Slack (1960) noted that the use of tape recordings for "research" in work with delinquents had the advantage that there was little stigma attached to talking for such a purpose. The delinquent does not have to play a patient role or accept the label of "patient." The delinquent does not feel coerced and does not have to admit that he needs help. Slack noted that the technique of paying the delinquent for his "research" participation can easily be extended. For example, delinquents can be paid to take psychological tests for research purposes which may then be used to further the psychologist's understanding of the delinquent. The ethics of such a procedure are, however, probably open to debate.

Steinberg et al. (1968) explored having clients talk into a tape recorder by themselves and compared the effects of no feedback versus giving the client three minutes of feedback before each session, together with indirect suggestions as to what they should focus on in the session. No differences were found in the openness, discussion of self, expression of feelings, and guardedness of the two groups of clients. Those clients given feedback, however, showed a significant increase in long pauses, indicating that feedback inhibited the flow of speech. Steinberg et al. suggested that the feedback made the therapist seem more evaluative and that this inhibited the clients.

Slack and Slack (1972) had people talk into a tape recorder

which had a counter that clicked as long as they talked and tallied the clicks. When they were silent, the counter stopped tallying. The volunteers were paid on the basis of the final tally on the counter. The volunteers reported feeling better after their monologues with the tape recorder, and Slack and Slack noted that portions of their monologues were highly personal and similar to interpersonal interviews.

Stollak and Guerney noted that the feedback to the patients could be increased, and this might facilitate psychotherapeutic movement. Stollak and Guerney saw their technique as useful for screening patients for their motivation for psychotherapy and for examining their aptitude for psychotherapy. The technique could also be used to introduce clients to psychotherapy (by building up their positive transference toward the psychotherapist, for example, prior to beginning psychotherapy proper).

DISCUSSION

Maslow (personal communication) has reported an experience similar to those described above. He had clients go into a room by themselves and talk into a tape recorder about whatever they wished for half an hour by themselves. They then played back the tape recording and listened to it. They did this regularly. Maslow reported that the clients noted an improvement in their psychological state as a result of this experience.

Here there is no psychotherapist. All that we have is the client talking out loud by himself. The client receives feedback, not from a trained psychotherapist but from himself. He hears what he himself has said some thirty minutes earlier. If this process is beneficial, what implications does it have for our understanding of psychotherapy?

It seems to suggest that the particular kind of feedback that the psychotherapist gives a client is not critical for the client to feel better. This conclusion was suspected when research studies suggested that all therapists, regardless of their particular theoretical orientation and treatment techniques, were successful in treating clients. It seemed that the presence of a warm, nonjudgmental, empathic person was all that was necessary. But it appears that even this may not be necessary. All that may be necessary is impersonal feedback, a monitoring of one's own behavior that one has never had before. This feedback can come from another person; it can also come from a tape recording of one's own spoken thoughts.

REFERENCES

Cautela, J.: Treatment of compulsive behavior by covert sensitization. *Psychol Rec, 16*:33-41, 1966.

Denholtz, M.: The use of tape recordings between therapy sessions. *J Beh Ther Exp Psychiat, 1*:139-134, 1970.

Denholtz, M. and Mann, E.: An automated audiovisual treatment of phobias administered by nonprofessionals. *J Behav Ther Exp Psychiatry, 6*:111-115, 1975.

Donner, L. and Guerney, B.: Automated group desensitization for test anxiety. *Behav Res Ther, 7*:1-13, 1969.

Heim, A. and Watts, K.: The Brook Reaction Test of interests. *Br J Psychol, 57*:171-185, 1966.

Henning, J., Levy, R., and Aderman, M.: Reliability of MMPI tape recorded and booklet administration. *J Clin Psychol, 28*:372-373, 1973.

Maslow, A.: *Motivation and Personality.* New York, Har-Row, 1970.

Migler, B. and Wolpe, J.: Automated self-desensitization. *Behav Res Ther, 5*:133-135,1967.

Schwitzgebel, R.: Delinquents with tape recorders. *New Society, 1(18)*:11-13,1963.

Schwitzgebel, R.: *Streetcorner Research.* Cambridge, Harvard Pr, 1964.

Slack, C.: Experimenter-subject psychotherapy. *Ment Hyg, 44*:238-256, 1960.

Slack, W. and Slack, C.: Patient-computer dialogue. *N Engl J Med, 286*:1304-1309, 1972.

Stampfl, T. and Levis, D.: Implosive therapy. *Behav Res Ther, 6*:31-36, 1968.

Steinberg, T., Guerney, B., and Stollak, G.: Autoanalytic behavior with and without suggestion and feedback. *Psychol Rep, 23*:1120, 1968.

Stollak, G. and Guerney, B.: Exploration of personal problems by juvenile delinquents under conditions of minimal reinforcement. *J Clin Psychol, 20*:279-283, 1964.

Urmer, A., Black, H., and Wendland, L.: A comparison of taped and booklet forms of the MMPI. *J Clin Psychol, 16*:33-34, 1960.

Chapter 6

EPILOGUE

THE previous chapters have presented a review of the various uses to which the different modes of communication have been put in counseling and psychotherapy. In addition to the detailing of these various uses, there have been comments on the changes that the use of these modes brings to the psychotherapeutic process. These changes are of importance and merit restatement here.

THE EFFECTS OF CHANGING THE MODE OF COMMUNICATION

Common to many of the modes is the result that their use equalizes the status of client and counselor. No longer does the counselor sit behind a desk in his office with the client opposite him. Especially with the use of telephone counseling, but also with the use of television and the printed word, each participant sits in his own environment transmitting only verbal cues, thereby eliminating differences in status observable through dress and furnishings.

A second effect is the equalization of power. In the use of the telephone or in Nathan's TRACCOM television system, the client can hang up or tune out the counselor and thereby has increased power over the counseling interaction. A number of recent writers have focussed on the power involved in the counseling relationship and its abuse by counselors. Halleck (1971) has perhaps been the most outspoken in warning of the dangers of indoctrination by the counselor and other abuses of power. The systems of communication described in this book alleviate the problem to some extent by giving the client some power too.

A number of features of altering the mode of communication may facilitate counseling. The possibility of remaining anonymous while talking to a counselor (via telephone or computer) and the possibility of richer fantasy concerning the counselor (positive transference) have been mentioned as facilitating self-disclosure and trust, at least in the earlier stages of counseling. The possibility that particular kinds of patients may benefit from the changed mode of communication has also been referred to in each chapter.

Many of the systems of counseling based upon changing the mode of communication have increased the accessibility of counseling, which is important for certain groups, such as the infirm and those in crisis. Counseling can also be more immediate, and the cost can be reduced. The client may not have to travel to the counseling center, for example, and a counselor (or computer) may be shared by a number of agencies or regions, thereby permitting more efficient use of his time.

RESTRICTING THE CUES IN COMMUNICATION

The use of alternative modes of communication cuts down the cues available for examination. The use of television reduces the richness of the communication least. In telephone counseling, all nonverbal cues are eliminated. Hilf, et al. (1971) eliminated some of the cues in verbal communication. They had the client and the counselor sit in different rooms, communicating via a teletype, thereby eliminating paralinguistic and nonverbal channels of communication. (The patient was told that the interview was being conducted by a computer.) This arrangement changed the tempo of the communication, though hesitations before responding were noticeable to the receiver. Some of the patients who used the system said that they felt that the interviews were of benefit to them. Hilf noted that the technique might be of use for mute patients and for training psychotherapists (since the trainee will have a transcript available for inspection and because the tempo of the psychotherapy is slowed down).

Some may object that the elimination of communication cues will impede effective counseling. However, the elimination of cues may be beneficial for some patients. For the client to talk to the counselor without being eyed by him may facilitate psychotherapeutic movement. After all, traditionally the psychoanalyst sits so that his patient cannot see him; the Catholic religion has chosen in the past to restrict communication cues in the confessional. Secondly, restricting the cues available in counseling may serve to make the counseling situation different from conventional talking and so may focus the participants more intently upon the task of counseling. In the discussion of telephone counseling, it was noted that the mode facilitates the degeneration of counseling into conversation. The system of communication devised by Hilf and his colleagues would minimize this distortion of the psychotherapeutic process. There is also some evidence that audio-audio communication is more effective in inducing opinion change if the person does not believe in the view that he is presenting (Michael Tyler, personal communication).

Occasional reports have confirmed the utility of reducing communication cues. Lowinger and Huston (1955) had patients and their psychotherapists sit in separate rooms so that they could hear but not see each other. Psychotherapy was quite effective. Eight of the ten patients were judged to have formed a transference relationship with the psychotherapist, but it was less intense in emotion than is customarily found. For example, none of the patients used the transference relationship to facilitate their resistance.

Two of the patients used the solitary situation to become more motorically active in the room. One even masturbated on one occasion. One patient reported that she found it easier to concentrate on her problems since she did not have to worry about getting involved with another person in the room. The psychotherapists found it easier to experience emotions such as fear, anger, sexual arousal, and boredom; they were able to express these emotions motorically since the patient could not see them.

DiMascio and Brooks (1961) found that patients in psychotherapy were able to develop a transference relationship with invisible, inaudible observers who were watching face-to-face psychotherapy sessions. They examined this phenomenon by asking a female patient to sit in a room twice a week and talk about her problems. She was told that a psychotherapist who did not know her and whom she did not know was watching her and listening to her via a one-way mirror. She was told that he would keep what she said completely confidential and she would never see or hear him. Once a week she saw her regular psychotherapist in a face-to-face session.

The patient felt reticent at first in the solitary sessions, but she soon became less inhibited. She developed a relationship with the unseen psychotherapist. She felt that he got to know her better. She personalized him and referred to him as "my therapist." She never doubted that he existed. She described him as being tall in her fantasy, with black wavy hair. She described the experience as similar to talking with God.

She also found the sessions of some use in helping her formulate her ideas before her regular psychotherapy sessions, and therefore saved time. Her psychotherapist agreed with her assessment of the solitary sessions.

One cannot conclude that these reduced forms of psychotherapy are as effective as traditional psychotherapy; although they may be, there are as yet little data on this issue. Martin et al. (1960) gave highly anxious people one of the following three tasks: (1) talking into a tape recorder by themselves; (2) talking to a psychotherapist who reinforced their talking nonverbally (by nodding or saying "uh-huh"); and (3) talking with a psychotherapist who responded in a natural fashion. Judges listened to the interviews, and their ratings indicated that the tape recorder group tended to avoid emotionally important material in succeeding sessions whereas the traditional psychotherapy group tended to deal with such material more and more. Also, anxiety levels seemed to rise more during the sessions with the tape recorder group than with the other groups.

Thus, it would appear that psychotherapeutic movement was less in those who talked to a tape recorder than in those in regular psychotherapy. However, this study did not examine alleviation of problems or happiness as a criterion. What might appear to be psychotherapeutic movement to the investigators (talking about emotionally important material in this case) might not have helped the subjects function any better in society.

Obviously, changing the system of communication for counseling is not appropriate for everyone. Those who have not been raised with telephones and television (such as the elderly, for example) will not find the use of these modes of communication easy; but others might. For example, autistic children may benefit from being removed psychologically from the counselor, and those in crisis may be better able to handle the disembodied voice of a telephone counselor.

ELIMINATING THE COUNSELOR

When there is a movement to the use of computer programs for counseling, the presence of the counselor is being minimized. When clients talk into tape recorders and are given no feedback, or when they write letters to a counselor who never responds, the counselor has been eliminated completely (except perhaps in the mind of the client). Sometimes the presence of a counselor can make a patient more disturbed. Patients may feel less pressured by having a computer administer a questionnaire; a computer is nonjudgmental and clients may take their time in responding to its questions. Certainly, in vocational guidance by computer, little may be lost in eliminating the counselor.

The advantage of slowing the tempor of counseling down (by the use of teletypes, for example) may include the promotion of better impulse control in the client and the encouragement of intellectual (or secondary process) thinking. In addition, there are some research data to indicate that a counselor may inhibit aspects of the psychotherapeutic process.

Colby (1961) paid students to think out loud and free associate while he sat in the room. He would occasionally ask a question (such as, "What did your father have against you?") or make an interpretation (such as "You can't concentrate because you're worried she might find another guy.") After some relevant remark of either category, he would remain silent for ten minutes or so. Colby found that his interpretations had a more facilitating effect on the free associations of the students than the questions. It would appear then that particular responses by the listener can facilitate free association more than other kinds of responses. Incidentally, all four students enjoyed the experience (which consisted of twelve half-hour sessions), and three found it psychotherapeutically helpful.

Colby (1960) examined the effects of the presence of an experimenter on a person's free associations. He paid students to free associate in a room by themselves while a tape recorder recorded their verbalizations. After four sessions, the experimenter would enter the room midway during the session and sit quietly there. All of the students reported a rise in tension and feelings of inhibition when the experimenter first entered the room, but these feelings decreased after a few minutes. Colby noted that the content of the free associations changed during his presence. During his presence, the number of references made to people (excluding himself) increased, particularly to male people. Thus, the presence of an experimenter changed the content of free associations.

Stigall (1966) had subjects talk while a television screen showed a listener who gave nonverbal reinforcement to the subject's talking. Other subjects received verbal reinforcement and other groups experienced these reinforcements with a live listener. The televised listeners were prerecorded. Both televised and live listeners increased the subjects' rate of talking. When verbal reinforcement was used, the live listener increased the rate of talking more than the televised listener. However, Stigall noted that though the rate of talking increased, the contingent social pressure of the live listener seemed to inhibit the free association of the subjects. Since the subjects appeared to expect a high rate of interaction with the live listener, their speech was influenced, thereby inhibiting the free association. So the presence of a psychotherapist may inhibit free association.

If talking to a tape recorder may have beneficial effects on a client, it would appear that the nonspecific effects of psychotherapy may be more substantial than had hitherto been realized. It has long been argued that the technique of psychotherapy utilized by the psychotherapist may be less important than the nonspecific features of the whole situation. If it happens that a client benefits as much from talking to a tape recorder (believing perhaps that someone will listen to it) or from talking by himself in a room believing that someone is watching, then it may be that the technique of therapy deserves less importance than has been attributed to it. The presence of the psychotherapist may be important only to provide a rationale for having a patient talk out loud about his problem. Any behavior by the psychotherapist may serve only to inhibit psychotherapeutic movement. After all, as Watts (1961) has argued, the aim of psychotherapy is to move the patient to the realization that there are no answers to be found for his problems. He must learn to live his life as he is and cease yearning to be other than he is.

REFERENCES

Colby, K.: Experiments on the effects of an observer's presence on the imago system during psychoanalytic free association. *Behav Sci,* 5:216-232, 1960.

Colby, K.: On the greater amplifying power of causal correlations over interrogative inputs on free association in an experimental psychoanalytic situation. *J Nerv Ment Dis,* 133:233-239, 1961.

DiMascio, A. and Brooks, G.: Free association to a fantasied psychotherapist. *Arch Gen Psychiatry,* 4:513-516, 1961.

Halleck, S.: *The Politics of Therapy.* New York, Science, 1971.

Hilf, F., Colby, K., Smith, D., Witner, W., and Hall, W.: Machine-mediated interviewing. *J Nerv Ment Dis,* 152:278-288, 1971.

Lowinger, P. and Huston, P.: Transference and the physical presence of the physician. *J Nerv Ment Dis,* 121:250-256, 1955.

Martin, B., Lundy, R., and Lewin, M.: Verbal and GSR responses in experimental interviews as a function of three degrees of "therapist" communication. *J Abnorm Soc Psychol,* 60:234-240, 1960.

Stigall, T.: Investigations in psychotherapy and verbal conditioning with conjugately programmed reinforcement. *Diss Abstr Int,* 27B:1631-1632, 1966.

Watts, A.: *Psychotherapy East and West.* New York, Random, 1961.

AUTHOR INDEX

A

Aderman, M., 99
Alston, E., 71, 90
Aronson, E., 76, 90

B

Bailey, K., 8, 11
Baizerman, M., 32, 39
Bannister, D., 90
Balance, W., 67
Bastein, S., 81, 90
Beebe, J., 19, 39
Beiser, M., 67
Bellino, T., 9, 11
Benfari, R., 44, 67
Black, H., 99
Bleach, G., 34, 39
Bloch, S., 90
Bloxom, A., 9, 13
Blum, L., 62, 67
Bonaparte, M., 90
Bringmann, W., 49, 67
Brockopp, G., 27, 30, 32, 35, 39, 40
Brooks, G., 102, 106
Brown, S., 90
Buchta, R., 34, 39
Burnell, G., 82, 90
Burton, A., 75, 82, 90
Butcher, J., 69
Butler, F., 39

C

Callis, R., 9, 12
Carothers, J., 34, 39
Cassel, R., 62, 67
Catanzaro, R., 7, 11, 20, 39
Cautela, J., 93, 99
Chase, J., 77, 90

Chick, J., 58, 59, 67
Chiles, J., 20, 39, 68
Christopher, P., 12
Claiborn, W., 34, 39
Clark, C., 11
Coddington, R., 45, 67
Coen, K., 67
Colby, K., 50, 52, 53, 55, 64, 67, 104, 105, 106
Cornelison, F., 7, 11
Cowan, C., 7, 11
Coyle, F., 68

D

Davidson, J., 81, 90
Davison, W., 12
Denholtz, M., 93, 94, 99
DiMascio, A., 102, 106
Dinoff, M., 6, 11
Donner, L., 49, 67, 95, 99
Dowds, J., 21, 40
Dunn, T., 47, 67
Dunphy, D., 69
Dwyer, T., 4, 11

E

Eberl, D., 9, 13
Enea, H., 55, 67
Elkins, G., 80, 90
Ellis, A., 71, 72, 75, 77, 90
Endicott, J., 44, 69
Evan, W., 47, 66, 67
Eysenck, H., 49, 67

F

Farber, J., 72, 90
Farrow, E., 70, 90
Forrest, D., 10, 11

Fowler, D., 34, 39
Fowler, R., 48, 49, 67, 68, 69
Freud, A., 90
Freud, S., 70, 90
Friedman, R., 46, 68
Friesen, D., 68
Fuller, D., 39

G

Games, R., 12
Gianturco, D., 43, 68
Giesbrecht, C., 67
Gilbert, J., 67
Glavin, R., 11
Glueck, B., 42, 69
Goldberg, I., 40
Gottschalk, L., 76, 90
Green, W., 20, 39
Greer, R., 9, 12
Greist, J., 25, 39, 45, 63, 66, 68
Grotjahn, M., 70, 90
Gruenberg, P., 8, 12
Gruver, G., 28, 39
Guerney, B., 49, 67, 95, 96, 99
Gustafson, D., 39, 68

H

Hall, W., 106
Halleck, S., 65, 68, 100, 106
Hansen, D., 68
Harris, J., 59, 61, 68
Harrower, M., 71, 90
Haworth, M., 9, 12
Hedl, J., 48, 68
Heim, A., 92, 99
Henning, J., 92, 99
Hershenson, D., 62, 68, 69
Higgins, W., 7, 12
Hilf, F., 55, 57, 67, 68, 101, 106
Himmelstein, H., 12
Hoff, L., 30, 39
Holtzman, W., 63, 68
Honigfeld, G., 42, 68
Hurst, R., 68
Huston, P., 102, 106

I

Impellitteri, J., 59, 68

Inslee, L., 34, 39
Itil, T., 8, 12
Ivey, A., 6, 12

J

Jacobs, A., 81, 90
Jennings, B., 28, 40

K

Kagan, N., 7, 12
Katz, M., 8, 12, 59, 68
Kelly, G., 75, 90
Kendra, J., 67
Kesen, S., 73, 90
Kew, C., 74, 90
Kinder, W., 7, 11
King, T., 45, 67
Kitchen, C., 68
Klein, D., 42, 68
Klein, M., 41, 68
Kleinmuntz, B., 43, 48, 49, 63, 68
Knights, R., 47, 68
Kochen, M., 68
Kora, T., 82, 87, 88, 89, 90
Koson, D., 47, 68
Krathwohl, D., 7, 12
Kris, E., 90
Krumboltz, J., 9, 12

L

Lamb, C., 28, 40
Lang, P., 68
Laughren, T., 39, 68
Leedy, J., 77, 90
Leighton, A., 67
Lester, D., 29, 30, 33, 35, 39, 40, 43, 67
Levis, D., 94, 99
Levy, R., 99
Lewin, M., 106
Likorish, J., 77, 90
Lind, J., 12
Lindsley, O., 4, 12
Liston, E., 12
Loehlin, J., 50, 51, 65, 68
Lorch, S., 69
Loughary, J., 59, 68

Lovaas, O., 66, 68
Lowinger, P., 102, 106
Lundy, R., 106
Lushene, R., 67

M

Macdonald, A., 9, 12
Macdonald, D., 8, 12
Mackinnon, R., 22, 24, 40
Mahoney, S., 77, 90
Mair, J., 76, 90
Mann, E., 94, 99
Marks, P., 48, 69
Marlowe, G., 68
Martin, B., 103, 106
Marvit, R., 8, 12
Maslow, A., 95, 98, 99
McCarty, G., 40
McColskey, A., 28, 40
McDonough, J., 33, 40
McGee, R., 28, 30, 34, 39, 40
McGuire, M., 55, 69
McKinney, F., 76, 90
McLaughlin, D., 12
Meehl, P., 57, 69
Melhus, G., 61, 69
Mendels, J., 43, 68
Menninger, W., 76, 90
Menolascino, F., 9, 12
Merritt, H., 11
Michels, R., 22, 24, 40
Migler, B., 93, 99
Miller, J., 47, 66, 67
Miller, W., 20, 24, 40
Mink, O., 12
Minor, F., 59, 69
Motelet, K., 82, 90
Mowrer, O., 10, 12
Myers, R., 69

N

Nathan, P., 3, 12, 100

O

Ogilvie, D., 69
Ohara, K., 82, 90

O'Neil, H., 67, 68
Owens, H., 20, 40

P

Paden, R., 9, 12
Paitich, D., 47, 69
Paul, G., 12
Pearce, K., 47, 69
Pearson, L., 90
Perdue, W., 67
Piotrowski, Z., 48, 69

Q

Quarton, G., 69

R

Rachman, S., 49, 67
Rader, G., 11, 12
Ramm, D., 43, 68
Rangell, L., 70, 90
Rathus, S., 9, 12
Reich, T., 39
Reitman, L., 11
Resnick, H., 9, 12
Richard, W., 30, 40
Robertiello, R., 19, 40
Rossi, M., 12
Rowse, G., 39, 68
Royce, J., 77, 90
Ryan, J., 11

S

Scheff, T., 32, 40
Schill, T., 11, 12
Schuyler, D., 12
Schwartz, E., 40
Schauble, P., 10, 13
Schwitzgebel, R., 95, 96, 99
Seeman, W., 48, 69
Shostrom E., 10, 12
Simmons, J., 66, 68
Simpson, R., 42, 69
Slack, C., 95, 97, 99
Slack, W., 45, 66, 69, 97, 99
Slaikeu, K., 34, 40

Smith, D., 106
Smith, M., 48, 69
Smith, R., 11, 66, 69
Smith, S., 12
Sowder, E., 8, 11
Spanier, D., 33, 40
Spitzer, R., 44, 69
Stampfl, T., 94, 99
Steinberg, T., 97, 99
Stevens, S., 68
Stigall, T., 105, 106
Stodolsky, D., 49, 53, 68, 69
Stollak, G., 96, 99
Stoller, F., 10, 13
Stone, P., 48, 69
Strauss, F., 39, 68
Striefel, S., 9, 13
Stroebel, C., 42, 69
Strupp, H., 9, 13
Stunden, A., 43, 69
Super, D., 69

T

Tapp, J., 33, 40
Thisted, R., 67
Thoresen, C., 12
Tiedman, D., 58, 69
Tulkin, S., 40
Tyler, M., 102

U

Uhlemann, M., 12

Urmer, A., 92, 99

V

Van Cura, L., 66, 68, 69
Varenhorsh, B., 12
Vermillion, M., 69

W

Waters, T., 6, 13
Watson, P., 47, 68
Watt, J., 67
Watts, A., 106
Watts, K., 92, 99
Wayne, G., 12
Webb, J., 49, 69
Weber, S., 67
Weizenbaum, J., 53, 55, 63, 65, 69
Wendland, L., 99
Wetzel, R., 39
Widroe, H., 81, 90
Williams, T., 21, 23, 33, 40
Wilmer, H., 5, 13
Witner, W., 106
Wolf, A., 20, 40
Wolpe, J., 93, 99
Woody, R., 10, 13

Y

Yalom, I., 78, 80, 90
Youst, D., 59, 60, 69

SUBJECT INDEX

A

Abortion counseling, 16
Accessibility, 14, 24, 101
Adolescents and children, 5, 7
Advice columns, 72
Alcoholics, 3, 7, 9, 16, 20
Anonymity, 14, 22, 101
Anonymous correspondance, 85
Anxiety, 21
Assertiveness training, 9
Autism, 50, 104

B

Behavior therapy, 20, 49, 93
Bibliotherapy, 76

C

Call for action, 17
Case reports, 42
Catharsis, 76, 84
Child abusing parents, 16
Chronic patients, 30, 35
Client-centered therapy, 53, 65
Computers, 41f
Confession, 10, 102
Confidentiality, 64
Consultation, 5, 17, 20, 84
Control by client, 21, 66, 100
Conversation, 26, 102
Correspondance therapy, 71f
Cost, 5, 24, 45, 61, 63, 101
Covert Sensitization, 93
Crisis intervention, 5, 14f, 101, 104

D

Deaf patients and therapists, 73, 83
Defense mechanisms, 4

Delinquents, 8, 62, 95
Depression, 21
Diagnosis, 9, 43
Diaries, 84, 88
Drug problems, 5, 16, 62

E

Effectiveness of counseling, 33
Emergencies, 5
Empathy, 28, 34, 77, 99
Ethics, 28, 46, 61, 63, 71, 97
Evaluation, psychiatric, 5
Evaluation of services, 33

F

Fixed-role therapy, 75
Flooding, 94
Follow-up of patients, 16
Free association, 6, 70, 74, 104

G

Group psychotherapy, 78f

H

Homicidal crises, 24, 43
Homosexuals, 16
Hypnosis, 20

I

IATV, 4
Implosive therapy, 94
Impulse control, 84, 104
Insight, 7
Interpersonal process recall, 7
Interpretation, 70
Interpretation of psychological tests, 48

Interviewing, 44
ISVD, 58

L

Legal issues, 65

M

Malingering, 9
Marriage counseling, 7
Matching client and counselor, 4, 43
Mentally retarded, 9
Microcounseling, 6
Modeling, 9, 94
Monologues, 5, 95
Morita therapy, 82, 87
Motor movement, 4
Mute patients, 101

N

Neurosis, 77, 81, 87
Nondirective therapy, 53, 65
Nonprofessional counselors, 27, 66, 95

O

Obscene callers, 29
Obsessive-compulsives, 26
Occupational therapist, 88
Outreach teams, 30

P

Paranoids, 5
Paraprofessional counselors, 27, 66, 95
Phobias, 22, 95
Planning, mental health, 46
Poetry therapy, 77
Poison information centers, 14
Power, 4, 21, 66, 100
Psychoanalysis, 19, 70, 102
Psychological testing, 11, 47, 92, 97

R

Rape counseling, 16
Rational emotive therapy, 77
Reading, 77
Records, 7, 41, 59
Regression, 6
Relaxation, 20, 93
Research, 6, 8, 33, 53, 71
Resistance, 70, 71, 74, 83, 97, 102
Rogerian therapy, 53, 65
Rumor control, 17

S

Schizophrenia, 5, 19, 25, 26, 81, 82
Selection of counselors, 33
Senior citizens, 15, 24, 104
Sensitivity groups, 9
Social class, 9
Spontaneous writing, 74
Status, 4, 21, 80, 100
Suicidal patients, 9, 23, 24
Suicide prediction, 33, 42, 43, 45
Suicide prevention, 14
Supervision, 8, 20
Symbolism, 77
Systematic desensitization, 10, 49, 93

T

Tape recording, 34, 92f
Teen hotlines, 15, 32
Telephones, 14f
Television, 3f
Textbooks videotape, 10
TRACCOM, 3
Training, 6, 46, 51, 101
Transference, 6, 19, 22, 70, 75, 82, 83, 95, 96, 98, 101, 102

V

Videotape, 3f
Vocational counseling, 9, 57, 93, 104

W

Writing, 70f

Z

Zen, 89